Table of Contents

Regarding James Shore (April, 1969-Oct, 2009)

James died in October of 2009. Right around the time we began to "shop" this book. We were very excited to finish it up, having spent several years working on it as time would allow. James's sudden passing left me wondering what exactly to do with the not-quite-finished tome. James was a substantial talent and an incredible mind. And his mastery of all-things SEM far surpassed my own. I thought hard on what to do with this treatise. The more I did, the more I became convinced that it had to see the "light of day."

I approached Tony Verre, a long-time friend and colleague of ours. When he heard about "the book" he volunteered to see to the unfinished threads that would have fallen to James to complete. This book could not have existed without Tony's expert knowledge, ability as a creative writer, and without his demonstrable human-ness.

The love for a dearly-departed friend is impossible to describe. I am not any closer to being able to verbalize the depth of loss or its profundity than when I first received the early-morning call. There are certain things we, the surviving, often would like to say to our departed loved ones. Things we wish we had said. But, alas, we cannot go back in time and say those things. What we can do is to honor them by seeing through to fruition unfinished business, to resolve the final notes of the song otherwise left hanging in the air begging for resolution.

I do know some things about deep affection for others. Much of it learned through 25 years of friendship with James. I know for sure is that he is well pleased this book has been finished. I know is he is proud of Tony's efforts to see through the completion of this book on his behalf. I know is that he is likewise proud that Tony (one of his former understudies) has developed into a real sharpshooter in the disciplines of search marketing. Finally, what I know is that while none can replace James, a man could not have a finer friend than Mr. Verre. Of course, James would find many things to change in this edition . . .beginning with my long-windedness.

In the end analysis, I would submit that no truer words have been spoken than these: "The language of love is sacrifice." James laid down his life so that another could live. His final moments were those of a hero. I give thanks to this man who has translated from this storyline to the next: In honor of his memory, in honor of friendship everywhere, in honor of his surviving wife and children, we offer this work of love.

God Bless James Shore. Loving father and husband. Beloved son and brother. Rest in the arms of God, my dearest friend. We persevere with you in mind and very much alive in the memory of our hearts.

Matt

Matt@SunAnt.com

Tony "don't call me Anthony" Verre and James "Hoffa" Shore, Summer 2009

P.S. *James would be shaking his head and saying, "Would you just shut up already and get on with it? Do you think these people have all day?" And that would set me to blathering on and on and on, just to really tweak him.*

Forward: Why Bother?

The advent of the Internet marks a dizzying tectonic shift which has transformed the 'System of the World.' It has revolutionized the way the world interacts with information in virtually every way. It has changed how we, as consumers, research, shop, interact, and make purchase decisions. As a result, the web has also changed the very nature of what effective marketing, sales, and client relationship management entail. Businesses today have no choice but continually to evaluate and align every aspect of their marketing, sales, and brand development in accordance with this new modality.

For businesses prepared to avail themselves, the Internet provides immediate access to exponentially greater insight into the proclivities of consumers, near limitless sales opportunities, an amazing array of real-time performance statistics, and the platform upon which to reach more than 6 billion prospects worldwide!

On the flip side, businesses that resist--choosing instead to continue operating upon outmoded 'sensibilities' and marketplace expectations of the last century--will find themselves moving ever more rapidly from the ICU to permanent life support in the coma ward.

The Internet, with its websites, search engines, social networking portals, exotic web and smart-phone applications, provides a direct-to-market sales channel greater than in any other medium. The web is like TV, radio, print, direct mailers, billboard advertising and more, all rolled into one. *What more could Marketing Professionals ask for?* The emergence of the Internet is a fantastic development for businesses, offering incalculable opportunities for profit.

Still, most executive decision-makers we encounter continue to struggle to understand the dynamic ins-and-outs of the online marketplace. While the business goals of the past remain unchanged (i.e., brand prosperity, recognition, and protection) the strategies to successfully achieve those goals are so radically altered as to be almost incomprehensible to those unfamiliar with the inner-workings of the web.

eProfitability is our attempt, as seasoned interactive veterans, to provide a clear understanding to executive decision-makers in this time of rapid change. Businesses that understand and adopt the eProfitability model will thrive. Those that do not will never realize the full potential of their marketing and sales efforts. Even in the face of today's financial crisis, the web will continue to thrive as our socio-technological evolution continues unabated. Just because the rules of strategic marketing have changed does not mean that the underlying 'Goal' of business has changed - far from it! Right now, there are more opportunities to make money, to maximize profit, than anyone dreamed possible only a few decades ago.

The Goal of any business is profit, to more money than you are spending. In Dr. Eliyahu M. Goldratt's best-selling and groundbreaking book, The Goal – A Process Of Ongoing Improvement, Goldratt puts this harsh but simple reality front and center. Essentially, Goldratt argues that profit is the only true manner in which a business can (or should) evaluate its progress and health. The more profit, the healthier the company. It is your job, then, as a business decision-maker to engage in high-return activities at the expense of relatively less-profitable endeavors. To do so, you must embrace the new reality of the *online market space* to the best of your ability. Applied eProfitability is one of the highest-return initiatives available to businesses today. Why? Because Applied eProfitability is relatively inexpensive, yet incredibly efficient. It is a business discipline in which modest, incremental changes can yield enormous bottom-line results.

Based on a quarter century of combined applied experience in the realms of interactive development, marketing, and management, the strategies detailed in this book will provide the direct means for you and your business to thrive in these exciting times. eProfitability professes a philosophical, conceptual, and practical foundation that will enable any decision-maker to seize and control the new opportunities offered online. In each chapter, we will guide you, illuminating common pitfalls, crucial best practices, and arming you with step-by-step implementation instructions on how to build a powerful and all-encompassing online marketing strategy.

After reading this book, you will have the knowledge, the tools, and the stats to create a *holistic interactive marketing* plan worthy of presentation to any Executive Board. Think of eProfitability as a *"Why and How to Succeed Online"* guidebook. Regardless of the size of your company, or what products and services you provide, this book promises to provide you with everything you need to flourish in today's online marketplace.

We hope you enjoy the ride!

James Shore and Matthew Collins
9/18/09

Chapter 1: The Basics of Applied eProfitability

Before we go into the details of how we can help you maximize the profitability of your business through building a *holistic interactive marketing plan*, we need to examine the defining relationships which give rise to an *ecosystem* which offers sustainable sales opportunities (leads) today and into the future. As you will see, the ecosystem we are describing is more complex than it might appear at the surface. A significant part of beginning to understand how to maximize your online presence is simply through appreciating the complexities and dynamics at work. So we start – at the beginning!

The eProfitability Wheel

What business book would be complete without a diagram like this one?

Figure 1: The eProfitability Wheel

As depicted in **the eProfitability Wheel**, the process begins with marketing and traffic, governed by website content, gains success through lead capture and lead conversion (sales), and is perpetuated through CRM to ensure a continuous flow of both returning and new users through the site.

Marketing & Traffic

The process begins with the end users and your ability to reach them. Obviously, traffic to your site is a defining component of online success. Without traffic, we have no visitors to turn into leads and no leads to convert to sales in the first place. However, 'traffic' is not a standardized entry in a spreadsheet. There are demographics and geo-locations of traffic; there are levels of *quality* of traffic, from the casual surfer to the purchaser ready-to-buy today; there are various sources of traffic, which in many cases determine the *quality* component; and there are unique/new versus returning users, each with distinct objectives when visiting your site. *Most business owners only consider the quantity of traffic, because they have neither the perspective to account for the varying qualities and types of users, nor the ability to respond appropriately and distinctly to each one's individual needs.*

eProfitability will cover the full array of online marketing opportunities that should be considered by any business serious about maximizing profit from their online efforts. How effectively you market yourself online will determine how much traffic you can obtain and is *one* of a series of important factors which governs the quanitity of leads your site churns out. And the more leads you have, the more opportunity you have to turn a greater profit.

In today's online *market space*, the single most important strategy is Search Engine Marketing (SEM). That is, Search Engine Optimization (SEO) and Pay-Per-Click advertising (PPC). All other online marketing tactics should be considered as complementary to these, the two pillars of online marketing. There is no doubt that blogs, Twitter, and YouTube can drive direct traffic to your site, but they can only be fully effective if they are implemented in proper relation to your SEM (SEO & PPC) efforts. The reasons for this go far beyond ranking considerations alone, but more on this later!

Website Content

Content, as you see from *Figure 1*, sits in the most prominent position at the top of the wheel. It is the *sine qua non* from which all online marketing strategies either succeed or fail. When we speak of "content," we mean it in the broadest sense of the term. *"Content" not only includes every aspect of your site that is dependent upon the use of words (textual content), but also images, multimedia, navigational elements, and site aesthetics.* So, in the context of eProfitability, when we say "content," we are speaking to *all* aspects of the website experience. A website is not merely a billboard!

Your website is not only the foundational element of your online presence; it is the cornerstone of your corporate image - of your business branding – online and offline. To be effective, *your website content must simultaneously 1) fulfill distinct user expectations, 2) satisfy requirements for a multitude of concurrent strategies, and 3) satisfy lead capture and/or online sales objectives.*

To make matters more complex, all website content needs to be framed, and in many cases *constrained*, by established norms of web design: learned conventions, demonstrable user preferences, and template limitations of today's website platforms. So, while "content" concerns itself *primarily* with the end user experience (usability), it must also meet corporate, marketing, and sales needs (maximizing profitability). This means, for example, that our analysis needs to extend beyond top-level messaging and calls-to-action to drive leads and sales. Our analysis needs to extend into the micro: considering the very specific verbiage used in order to drive the type of conversion event desired. Suffice to say for now, naming everything appropriately will not only help to heighten ranking in the search engines, it will also engage your audience by developing relevance between what they are looking for and your offerings.

In this book, we will explore the primary Content Considerations in relation to *Information*:

From the basic:

- Navigation
- Style
- Platform
- Sales Copy
- Keyword Integration

To the more complex:

- User Paths
- Calls to Action
- Landing Pages
- Internal Linking Structure
- Lead Capture and Conversion

Lead Capture (Traffic Conversion)

This is perhaps the least understood aspect of the eProfitability Wheel. Yet it is a crucial component of your online marketing success. Without discerning and integrating appropriate Lead Capture mechanisms, you are wasting every dollar you spend online. Traffic that we fail to convert into actionable leads (whether a form submission, phone call, or other Conversion Event) or a sales transaction gets us no closer to realizing profit than complete absence of traffic!

Lead Capture does not have to be obnoxious or overly-intrusive to be effective. But proper Lead Capture goes far beyond relying on the user to click on an embedded "contact us" link (which is statistically proven to be a lesson in fruitlessness). Likewise, expecting anyone nowadays to fill out a lengthy 20+ field form requiring every possible piece of personal contact information is sure to drive even the most promising potential opportunity away from your site and into the open arms of a competitor, if merely from spite.

Lead Capture, for our intention, can be defined as a *Conversion Event resulting in the acquisition of just enough information to start a "conversation" with a prospective customer.* In most cases, site publishers don't need loads of personal data up front, but rather a name, email, and in some cases a phone number, giving the site visitor the opportunity to submit a quick inquiry. With the exception of eCommerce models and sites which require detailed applications (i.e. for Insurance, financial service accounts, etc.), the only objective should be to capture just enough information to establish a relationship and start a conversation.

Lead Capture is achieved by providing clear calls-to-action on most if not all pages of your site. Strategic and tasteful use of incentive-driven Lead Capture mechanisms should also be considered, as when properly implemented they offer incredible results. Put down the baseball bat and stop trying to "smash the monkey." A gentle nudge with the right incentive and transparent offer of free exchange will go a long way to converting anonymous traffic into qualified leads. *All you have to do is **ask in the right way**, and users will let you know who they are and why they are visiting your site.* The best part about effective on-site Lead Capture strategies is that business is not relying on 3rd party sources for lower-quality leads. Instead, the business is capturing self-qualified leads: prospective clients who are already on your site as anonymous users!

Lead Conversion (Sales)

We have separated Lead Conversion (converting a lead into a sale) from Lead Capture (converting traffic into a lead) because they are two distinct aspects of the eProfitability process (unless we are speaking of eCommerce models). As such, each must be dealt with and accounted for independently. A Lead Conversion (sale) can only happen once a lead has been captured – and the lead contact information is in hand. This is obvious. However, the Internet has once again redefined the expectation of the public. Days, even hours, of lag time before an initial direct "touch" (response) has been made can prove fatal.

Internet savvy customers who make the effort to express their interest in a given product or service (providing contact data in the form of an online lead) expect an *immediate and personal* response.

Over the years, we have seen time and time again incredible leaps in sales conversion ratios when the effort is made to follow up with leads within seconds or minutes of submission. One of the best impressions you can make as a company that cares about its clients is to engage each lead immediately and appropriately. The goal (though not always attainable) should always be to engage the lead while they are still surfing your website.

Lead Conversion should be the easiest step in the process. Why? Because the user has come to your site, provided you with their contact information, and in so doing have pre-qualified themselves . . . simply waiting for you to close the deal! Being aggressive in terms of following up with leads does not require setting a bulldog sales team member on every lead like used car salesman that makes you regret setting foot on the car lot. What it does require is an *immediate* response. But responsiveness is only one important factor driving successful Lead Conversion. The response also has to be appropriate. If the lead provides his/her phone number, a phone call *is* warranted. If the lead provides his/her email and phone number, but indicates a preference for email, then follow-up with an actual human-crafted email, not just a generic auto-responder! The response, whether by phone or email (or snail-mail for that matter) needs to do a couple things: 1) speak to the lead's specific inquiry (re: the reason they are contacting you), 2) describe next steps in the process (set appropriate expectations). Preferably then, first contact will be made by someone with the knowledge to answer specific questions about the product/service, and either close the deal on the spot or schedule a follow up appointment.

Clearly, then, not all leads need to be or should be treated alike. *Whether someone is ready to close today, or in 6 months, they constitute a viable lead that must be handled appropriately.* We insist that *every lead is a viable lead*, even though the idea is controversial. Many salespeople are only concerned with their next paycheck and do not have the proper long-range perspective or incentive to handle a potential client who might not be ready to close for weeks or months to come. All too often we have heard the self-defeating mantra "internet leads are garbage." To any who cling to this belief, we would respond, "The only thing that is garbage is your lead conversion and lead management process."

Which brings us to CRM.

CRM

Customer Relationship Management (CRM) is the bedrock of your business. Initially pertaining almost entirely to maximizing existing client relationships, CRM has come to mean much, much more. *CRM in its current form not only concerns itself with existing clientele, but also sales lead management (steering potential customer leads properly toward the end of more closed deals), and even into project/process management.* A more appropriate acronym would be LRM: Lead Relationship Management. But since we are unlikely to win that battle, we'll stick with referring to it as "CRM."

Today's marketplace offers tons of options in terms of CRM solutions, from Salesforce.com to Open Source CRM solutions like SugarCRM.com. What successful businesses have come to understand is that *just because a lead doesn't close today, doesn't mean it won't close tomorrow* (or in 3 months or a year from now). Because future *profits are at stake*, it is critical for your business to have a CRM Solution *and* a CRM Process in place to manage the often-tedious practice of lead follow-up properly. Implementing an effective CRM system can be *the determining factor* in your company's success. As the business owner, or senior manager, you need to know how effective your sales team is at closing deals and maintaining the follow-up "touch" cycle. The only way to know is with a system that tracks everything (to a degree, of course) they do and provides that data in meaningful stats and reports that can drive continual improvement.

In the <u>eProfitability</u> Wheel, we see that the initial sale/conversion is far from the end of the opportunity. Your website will provide the launch pad for an ongoing relationship with every satisfied client. This is more than providing them with a 'Red Carpet Customer Care' experience; this means giving them reasons to keep coming back for more. Newsletters, email campaigns with value-added copy, and most importantly new and exciting content on your website, will all serve to keep the fire kindled for a warm relationship. Additionally, CRM is an invaluable requirement to maintaining healthy relationships with your existing clientele. The oft-cited saying, "The easiest sale to close is with a repeat customer," holds true. *Having an efficient CRM solution is critical; otherwise prospects and clients alike will remain largely untapped as unrealized opportunities for maximum profit.*

The Importance of Asking the Right Question

When a prospective client tells us "we want more leads from our web site," we start probing to find out what they actually mean by this statement. In **all** cases we find what is **actually** meant by this request is that the prospect is looking for more transactions and transaction-related revenue (no real surprise there). So, the client seems to understand that there is a relation between quantity of leads and sales and revenue resulting from sales. The desire for "more leads" is due to an intrinsic value in leads *per se*. But capturing more leads is not equivalent to converting more leads into sales. Rather, each lead's value is its potential to turn into a sale. It is true: the more leads you have, the more potential sales transactions you have. But potential doesn't pay the bills or payroll. What we really want is profit from sales transactions. At an intuitive level, our clients understand the world like this:

more leads = more sales

When in fact, the world works like this:

more leads = more potential sales transactions

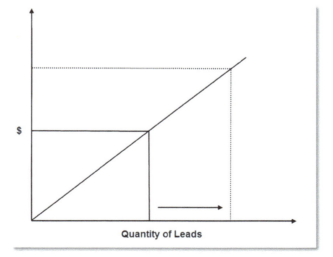

Quantity of Leads

Figure 2: Quantity of Leads to Realized Profit

Even so, all things being equal, the more leads you capture, the more transactions you can *expect*. That is, if you close 10% of all leads captured and double the amount of captured leads without changing how you go about converting those leads, you can *expect* to double your sales. But there is no guarantee that this is so, because in and of itself, getting more leads means nothing in terms of profit if we don't close more sales. So, when we speak of "wanting more leads," it would be *more appropriate* to say we are looking to increase sales revenue, so that we acknowledge that the world works more like this:

*more leads = more potential sales transactions = more Lead Conversions = **increased sales revenue***

Further, if we really want to be *100% accurate*, we would say "we want to increase the net profit from, or through, our website (since sales-related revenue and net profit are often found to be distinct)." Borrowing from Eliyahu M. Goldratt's *The Goal*, the Goal of any business is to maximize profit. If we agree on this principle, then we would not say "we want more leads from our website," when what we really intend to say is "**we want to maximize the profitability of our website**." While this may sound academic, it is more important than just a semantic correction. Restating the desired outcome in this manner (from "we want more leads" to "we want to maximize our profitability") is meant to focus us squarely on "The Goal" and the purpose of all corporations: *to realize profit*.

Why is this an essential distinction?

- The Website is *currently* the foundation, the primary platform, for driving all Interactive (online) Marketing campaigns.
- The only purpose of a corporate website is to drive lead conversion opportunities and to increase profit – period. Pretty pictures, professionally written content, multimedia and dynamic interactions exist only to serve this singular requirement.
- Focusing on the Goal allows us to develop effective strategies to attain it, while simultaneously integrating corrective measures, as necessary, to keep us squarely on target.
- As humans, we create reality based on belief systems and the focal points of our attention. Therefore, the acquisition of 'more leads' is a distraction from our true intention, the acquisition of wealth. In business terms: more profit.

Any analysis of how businesses should proceed with regard to Interactive Marketing should *always pivot on how best and most efficiently to accomplish the objective of **maximizing profits***. Without keeping this Goal in mind, the Internet can quickly turn into a resource-swallowing bottomless pit dedicated to chasing phantom "opportunities." Stating "we want more leads," when the actual objective is to maximize profitability, is substituting the means for the Goal, which is distracting. Therefore, the question to pose your Interactive Marketing vendor is this:

*"**Our goal is to maximize the profitability of our website. How can you help us achieve this Goal?**"*

To this we would respond, *"You have come to the right place. Pull up a chair. Let's evaluate your project!"*

The Importance of Analytics – The Hub

Analytics is the hub of the eProfitability Wheel, because without it, we have no compass to guide 'the ship' and are beholden to the winds of fancy, dead reckoning, and whim. Properly configured (set-up) and managed correctly, web analytics software provides marketers with insights that no other tools can. Web analytics software provides access to detailed statistics that allow us to optimize, reconfigure, and tweak our marketing efforts to maximize the benefit from any promotion or campaign.

Forget about waiting for months to evaluate variations in sales or leads. We can make real-time improvements within days, even hours in some cases. With the analytics tool of choice, you can have instant insight into everything that is happening with your website and marketing campaigns:

- Where your traffic is coming from
- The keywords used to find your site from search engines
- How well your site is performing
- What percentage of traffic is converting to leads
- How much revenue is generated

– and that's *just for starters*.

Today, all analytics systems collect data from web users in the same basic manner – through Javascript tracking code snippets that attach themselves to the user's web browser, a.k.a. "cookies." These cookies then register every action the user takes on the site. In the past, this tracking was accomplished through server logs, which proved to be tedious to manage and unreliable, because they required extensive set-up and management to obtain accurate data. The newer analytics systems are, for the most part, 'plug and play.' Keep in mind that no system is perfect and 100% accurate, and there will always be inherent weaknesses. For example, high security settings on a browser will block cookies. However, in most cases it is not an issue, as few web users crank their browsing security to such an extent (it impedes the online surfing experience and many of their favorite online applications require the user to accept cookies to use them). Many sites require cookies to be 'turned on' to display data (pages). Most, if not all, modern tracking systems use cookies due to their facilitating nature - they are easy to insert and provide consistent results.

Google has provided their free tool, Google Analytics, for many years now. It is extremely powerful, effective, and is sufficient for most businesses. However, there are multiple subscription-based services that do provide superior customization, tracking, and reporting. Among these suites, Omniture, Core Metrics, Urchin, and WebTrends are some of the best. However, unless you are running a high-volume eCommerce website or require very advanced reporting functionalities, there is typically very little need to pay for one of these more robust analytics systems. Especially when Google Analytics is free.

Web integration of Google Analytics is simple and fast. A quick upload of the code snippet onto the pages of your site is all it takes. Usually, this can be accomplished by adding it to the "global footer" of the site, which means the code is added into only one file and is then populated across all site pages (or *globally*), assuming your site has a global footer. Regardless, you or your webmaster can easily add this tracking code to your site within minutes. Then, it is merely a matter of waiting for the data to be collected – within a day you will be able to begin to understand your site, what works and what doesn't in the context of maximizing profitability, at a micro-level.

Details of your site and marketing campaigns, where your consumers come from and how they interact with your site, will unfold before your eyes, in a "dashboard" reporting center that can instantly provide you with just about anything you would want to know.

A small piece of advice – if it's not already on your current website, get Google Analytics integrated immediately! Put down this book and see to it this instant. Even if you don't know how to use it, start collecting the data ASAP – once your done with this book you will have a working knowledge of which stats are most important, and what to be aware of, for your web marketing success.

The Importance of Defining Success

How does one define success with any marketing campaign? Inevitably, most people you ask will provide a different set of criteria to evaluate your campaign against. Once again, this is an aspect of the marketplace's infancy and lack of standards. If you asked an SEO Specialist, they would respond "more traffic and higher rankings." If you ask a Social Media Specialist, they will tell you "the amount, or increase, of viral visibility. " Or perhaps it's a ratio of "tweets, Click-Through Rates, and effervescent brand buzz"(whatever that means). In the end, none of these answers is correct. They may provide the statistical parameters to logically support a supposition, but they are not direct indicators of success. They are metrics, to be sure. But they are not the Goal.

As an industry, it is imperative that all online marketing efforts be held to the same evaluation standards as traditional marketing has been in the past. We sometimes wonder if the current state of obfuscation is not intentional. It certainly serves the litany of independent specialists and agencies alike, with plenty of wiggle room to justify their budgets, and very existence. Within the echo of "Web 2.0," "Social Network Marketing," or even "Search Engine Marketing," rarely will you hear "to be held accountable against Sales, Leads, and/or Conversion Events." The solution is quite simple. Any and every campaign should be able to meet the following requirements to be considered successful. **S.A.R.C.** is what matters:

- **S**ales Increase – Did the effort drive sales and/or quantity of Lead Conversions?
- **A**ccountability – Using analytics and stats, can you definitively credit Lead Conversion activity, the results, to the campaign?
- **R**epetition – Are the results repeatable, or just a one-off statistical exception?
- **C**ost – Is the resultant Cost Per Lead, or Cost Per Close, competitive?

The Importance of Continual Improvement

With any concerted marketing effort, it is not enough to just reach a plateau and stop. There will always be room for improvement and room to expand. The object here is to not merely maintain a certain position or a certain number of Lead Conversions (sales). One must have the objective of continually growing, for in business, stasis is death. In nature, all things exist in either one of two states: growth and expansion, or contraction and death. The same is true for business, especially as it relates to the online environment. Why? Because there are numerous competitors biting at your ankles ready to exploit any weakness, and the internet provides a venue for unlimited competition. This is a double-edged sword, for it simultaneously provides the opportunity for unlimited growth potential to all businesses alike. Big and small. Market giant and market twerp alike.

There are numerous metrics one can use to evaluate current effectiveness, growth, and the continual improvement of your web presence. However, we would propose that, in the end, only these few matter:

- Increasing Visibility which results in improved **Traffic Quantity**
- The refinement of targeting and messaging to improve **Traffic Quality**
- Increasing your onsite **Lead Capture Ratio**, while
- Decreasing **Cost Per Lead Conversion (Cost per Sale)**

'The Goal' is to increase profit. Therefore, focusing on these four objectives will keep you on the track to success. As you will discover by reading this book, these factors work synergistically together. The strategies we present will often times affect multiple objectives at the same time. Do not let yourself get distracted from these factors which matter most, as there will always be competing interests and information to divert your attention.

Summary

As a final note, Applied eProfitability is a *holistic* process that perpetually drives refinement of your entire online presence. From your website, to offsite marketing and promotional campaigns, as well as your core business objectives, we need to evaluate everything that is integral to your ability to sell your product or service. The following chapters will provide a detailed step-by-step explanation of how to do this, with instructions for using the requisite assessment tools, allowing you not only to understand the evaluation process, but effectively to appraise your company with your executive team in order to implement corrective measures to keep you on track (deep breath). You will find that many subjects are touched upon multiple times in different chapters. This is intentional and necessary. It is always easier to understand something when it is in reference to concrete applications.

Wow, that was a mouthful! Just keep in mind that the information presented in this book took more than two decades of combined experience to aggregate. It will take time to digest and interpret everything into a useful paradigm for you. We would strongly encourage you to read each chapter at least twice. We guarantee there will be multiple details you will better understand with the extra effort. The following chapters are presented in order of implementation for easier assimilation. IHowever, the order of the chapters and the steps in each chapter have been laid out carefully to provide a meaningful flow. As you will see, it is necessary to provide the theoretical foundation before divulging the practical application instructions. Without a clear understanding of "why," it is more difficult to grasp the "how." We strongly recommend completing each chapter before moving to the next, as the knowledge from the one extends through to and enhances the understanding of the next.

Progression of the Book

In order for us to reach the point where we are ready to cover the actual development of a profitable website and marketing campaign, we need to start with Lead Maximization Theory, a core aspect of the Applied eProfitability approach. Think of Lead Maximization Theory as the microcosmic laws governing the quantity of leads yielded by any given website.

From there, we will dive directly into detailing the myriad strategies for generating maximum profit from your website, boiling the massive subject to its most essential constituent parts (to the best of our ability) and imparting to you the core knowledge of how to achieve optimal success in a step-by-step, methodical manner.

A note: In many cases complete re-development of an existing website and marketing campaign will not be possible. We are not suggesting this is a requirement. The only requirement is your desire to improve what you're currently doing. Most if not all of the strategies we will outline in the book can be implemented into an existing program, and they will improve your current results and ROI. However, you should know that it is always easier to build a new palace than refurbish a dilapidated one. In some cases complete revamps will be necessary in order to move forward, particularly with websites that look like they were designed in 1985 on a Commadore 64. Realistically, we would ask, "is it really worth the expense and effort to drive traffic to such a site?" In most cases the answer will be "no." *Don't spend time and money on marketing when your website is either not likely to result in quantifiably more profit or, worse, likely to cost you potential sales!*

Chapter 2: Lead Maximization Theory

Lead Maximization Theory (LMT) is nothing more than a logical presentation of the obvious. Specifically it is **maximizing the quantity of leads captured from a given website** as a function, or an interplay, of variables beyond (but including) the sheer volume of *traffic* a site receives. But, in reality, even though we invented Lead Maximization Theory when we coined the term and began developing it in 2004, LMT still misses the larger point of this book. *True eProfitability isn't about quantity (or even quality) of leads. True eProfitability is about maximizing profit.* After all, leads (even high-quality ones) are worthless if they are not closed (converted). Nonetheless, Lead Maximization Theory is very useful as a primer – a good place to start a high-level discussion regarding how a website and the greater *metaverse* that is the Internet must be harmonized to maximize the potential sales transactions to be had.

The Mechanics of Lead Maximization Theory

To understand how to maximize the quantity of leads captured by a given website, one must first understand the theory behind it: what we like to call *the mechanical economy of lead maximization (or Lead Maximization Theory)*. Essentially, Lead Maximization Theory is a set of truisms. Similar to Geometry Theorems, Lead Max "Theorems" define a set of assumptions and then a corresponding equation and diagram demonstrating the relationships between variables. For most of us, it has been a while since having to struggle with geometry. We'll go slowly, because there is a real, tangible, and meaningful stuff herein for anyone with a website.

Lead Capture Ratio – the average amount of traffic your site must receive in order to generate one lead.

For example, if you average one lead for every 238 visitors, your Lead Capture Ratio would be 238:1 (or .42%)

The math looks like this:

```
238 hits        1 lead
-----    =    -----
 100%           x


Cross multiply:
238 * x = 100 * 1

238x = 100

Solving for variable 'x'.

Divide each side by '238'.
x = 0.42
```

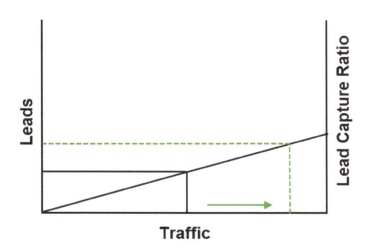

When people are looking to get more leads, they typically default to their intuitive sense that, *all things being equal, the more traffic that a given site gets, the more leads the site will generate.*

The mechanics of why this is true are represented above. As traffic goes up, leads go up as well - *even when the Lead Capture Ratio remains the same.* So, if we double the traffic to our site to 776 visitors and do nothing else, the site will generate, on average, 2 leads instead of one. If we triple the traffic, we will receive 3 leads, and so on.

This is why Search Engine Marketing works – *because if you change nothing about your site at all and drive more traffic to the site, you will receive more leads.*

But there is another, less-popular approach to increasing the leads you receive from your website. Examining the chart to the right, we can see that *if we increase our Lead Capture Ratio and leave our web traffic numbers untouched, we will receive more leads.* As such, *if we double our Lead Capture Ratio to .84 and the number of visitors the site receives remains unchanged at 238, the site will now generate, on average, 2 leads.*

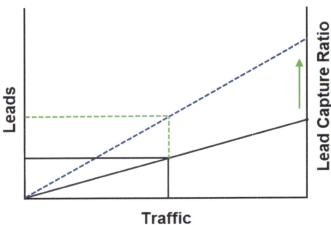

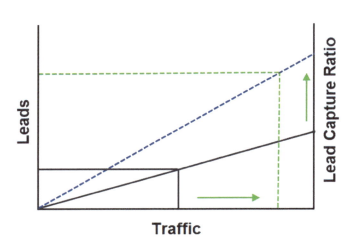

Of course, these are not mutually exclusive options. In fact, as demonstrated by the adjacent diagram, there is good reason to attempt both objectives (driving more traffic while also increasing your site's Lead Capture ratio) simultaneously. By doing both in tandem with one-another, the results of each is enhanced. Driving more traffic to a site with a low Lead Capture Ratio will result in capturing more leads – but not as many as would be captured if we had invested the time in cranking up our Lead Capture Ratio at the same time. Likewise, increasing our Lead Capture Ratio is great in and of itself – but not near as great as cranking up our traffic alongside out Lead Capture improvements.

Lead Max & Your Web ROI – Lead Maximization Applied

In light of the Goal, it is important to stress that the "art" and/or "science" of Lead Maximization is only recommended when it makes sense to apply it. And by that we mean, if there is an activity that offers a higher ROI than that offered by applying the principles of Lead Maximization Theory, by all means we would urge you to do that (whatever that may be) first! This is because adherence to the Goal means that we are obligated to pursue those activities which yield the greatest net profit.

Lead Maximization is never applied in a vacuum. It should be applied only when it makes good sense to do so--and when the context is right (i.e. your budget, the disposition of your site, your other web initiatives, your overall business initiatives, print initiatives, your personnel, advertising initiatives, SEO and PPC). What we will say is this: it is exceedingly rare to find a Client who cannot benefit immensely from applying Lead Maximization best practices.

Now, before you say, "I am convinced, let's do it," we have to remind you of The Goal! And here is why: depending on your situation--the product or service you sell, the competitive landscape online, the disposition of your current website, and your preparedness/ability to convert the leads you get from your website-- depending on these factors, among others, it may make more sense to focus on one objective over the other. It might make sense, in some cases, to put all of your efforts into driving more traffic. Or, it might make sense at this time to devote all of your immediate efforts on increasing your Lead Capture Ratio.

Here's what we mean: let's say you have $2000 to spend. You come to us and say, "I have $2000 to spend. And I can't wait to spend it on improving my web ROI." Hey, we are allowed to dream, are we not? Okay. So, we take a look at your site and find that . . . well, we find that there is a substantial amount of improvement to be made toward the end of improving your Lead Capture Ratio. We also find that your site is ranking fairly well in the search engines for the keywords (terms) that people looking for your services are using to search for them. It seems your web vendor has done a pretty decent job of the basics as far as Search Engine Optimization is concerned. Nonetheless, we also research the PPC opportunity and what $2000 is likely to yield for you as far as a return. What we find is that you are in an incredibly competitive market (which comes as no news to you). So, we recommend you to avoid PPC for now and invest your budget in improving your Lead Capture Ratio.

The point we are making is that when considering budgets and where to spend your money, it is crucial not to do so in a vacuum. No matter how much you have to devote to increasing your web ROI, it is crucial to work with a company that is going to spend your money wisely. And each case is unique, requiring professional research and analysis.

If you go to a company that focuses on Search Engine Optimization, they will usually try their best to sell you SEO, even if SEO is decidedly not where your money is best spent. Likewise, if you approach a PPC shop, they will push you towards PPC. When is the last time you visited a car dealership and they tried to sell you a motorcycle?

Similarly, let's say you approach an agency that has never even heard of Lead Maximization Theory," the terms "Lead Capture Ratio," or "Lead Capture Optimization." Yet you notice they offer top-notch design services as well as SEO and PPC (even though in the real world agencies are terrible at SEM in general). What is the likelihood they are going to know where your money is best spent? They have no overarching perspective from which to even evaluate where you will get the most bang for your buck, much less recommend the best path for you to take to increase your web ROI.

The Goal is to make money. This means you need to make sure you are spending your resources on those activities which offer highest-return. Anything less is detrimental to the health of your business.

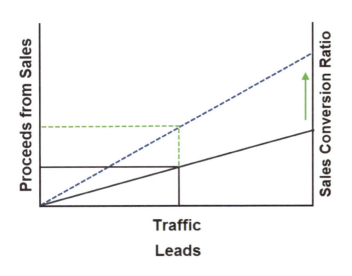

So before we get too far, we need to extend the discussion from a strict *quantity of leads* captured sense to one that relates directly to eProfitability specifically. If the Goal is maximum profitability, then we would be remiss not to state the following loudly and clearly:

Presuming your site has decent traffic and is capturing leads, *all things being equal, increasing your leads captured to sales conversion ratio will result in more sales-related dollars. And assuming that you are not selling at a net loss, increased profits will result.*

Now imagine a scenario in which we crank the traffic, crank the Lead Capture Ratio, crank the Sales Conversion Ratio, while also reducing our sales-related cost per sale. That is what we are aiming for with eProfitability.

Chapter 3: Online Strategic Marketing and Traffic

The first question we think anyone will ask us is, "Why start here? Why start with Strategic Marketing and not with the development of the website and website content?" Well, it's not only because the eProfitability Wheel starts with marketing, it's because you first need to understand the basics of online marketing in order to properly develop your content in such a manner as to efficiently drive traffic to your site, capture leads, make sales, and build revenue.

To use an analogy from real estate, "It's all about location and curbside appeal." Your website has to meet the needs, requirements and expectations of your target audience(s) to be effective, just as a real estate listing must in order to sell. As we will discuss in later chapters, websites must meet the requirements of each *distinct user type* and fulfill each type's often *distinct reasons* for visiting your site. This does not have to be an adversarial situation, but it is important to realize that more often than not, different people will have different standards and place different expectations upon the website.

Regardless of what anyone else says or wants, the only reason your website exists is to drive sales revenue. So, everyone else's interests aside, your website must primarily serve your paying audience-- that means prospects and clients first. Secondary user groups have to take second place in your mind, whether they are marketing people, sales reps, distributors, executives, or shareholders. How to best accomplish that small miracle will likely be a conversation that unfolds on a regular basis. However, having a clear understanding of how your marketing efforts will drive traffic to the site and directly impact your ability to convert that traffic into viable leads is critical before we begin the discussion of how to build an effective website.

Contrary to popular belief, these are not separate issues. *Online, your website and your marketing efforts must function as a seamless whole--in total harmony--to maximize profitability.* Our purpose is to provide you the perspective and tools you need to assess the best ways to achieve your sales and marketing objectives through the internet.

In this chapter we will provide a high-level analysis of the most important online marketing strategies. Most of them will be fleshed out in greater detail in later chapters. For our purposes, we are primarily concerned with marketing campaigns that directly result in website traffic. In the strict context of Online Strategic Marketing, traffic and the associated expenses are really the only metrics that matter. If we cannot statistically account for an effect of marketing, then it cannot be used as criterion of success. In other words, we cannot evaluate the impact that brand-awareness or brand-trust has on your business unless it is converted into the direct benefit of getting visitors to your website. Additionally, we have to be able to create a Cost-Per-Conversion value for the traffic and the sale, in order to evaluate ROI. Without this information, we don't have the ability to build a strategy or take corrective measures to improve our results.

Because of the importance and complexity of SEM (search engine marketing), the second half of this chapter is dedicated entirely to this subject. For now it is enough to state that *SEM will be the cornerstone of all your marketing efforts.* There is simply no way around this fact. We are all well aware that the Internet has single-handedly revolutionized the way commerce happens, both online and off. Regardless of your product or service, regardless of your target audience, the Internet has become everyone's research tool of choice. For the foreseeable future, the search engines have established themselves as the dominant interface for pursuing the product research process, whether the sale event is closed online or not.

Search engines are the gateway for 80-90% of global user interaction with the web, and more than 70% of respondents indicate that they do their research online before they make a purchase. Just ask yourself, when you want to find something where do you look? Most people under that age of 40 don't even own a land-line anymore; much less use the phone book. If you want your company to be found, you have to be listed in the search engines. Being listed on the first 2 pages of search results for your relevant keywords will provide the *highest quantity and quality* of traffic online. As you will see, SEM provides the best marketing ROI available, bar none.

To this end, all other forms of advertising should and can be structured to support your SEM strategies. Keep in mind that ranking and search exposure is not solely dependent upon your website: it's also determined to a very large extent by how your site is connected to the rest of the web.

Banner Advertising

Everyone knows what banner ads are – the often animated, graphical advertisements distributed across the web. They are most often encountered on general information websites like blogs and news sites, where the provider is not offering their own product or service line. Only sites that are not concerned about losing your attention, and thus sale, are going to display banner ads, in our estimation.

Statistically speaking, ever since the late 90's, banner ads have been considered 'dead'. Before the search engines had established their dominance, and the PPC (pay per click) ad model was created by Google, banners were one of the few advertising opportunities available online. However, the marketplace was quickly saturated with ads that no one wanted to look at. *The internet is an antidote to the push marketing model, not an enabler of that same archaic model.* Like television commercials, consumers quickly became largely "immune" to the presence of banner advertisements. Most are completely ignored, if not blocked outright with browser plug-ins. This is known as "banner blindness." For a traffic-building strategy, banner ads are dead-ends. According for Forester Research, **a well-placed banner will convert less than 1% of users**. Talk about banner blindness!

This is not to say that we are completely against them. Utilized correctly, they are great for building brand-awareness online. Traditional marketing studies conducted over many decades prove conclusively that we as consumers subconsciously pick up and remember advertisements and brand names whether we are paying attention or not. So, if your company can afford to build its brand online, go for it. If your intention is to drive traffic and create quality leads, your money is better spent elsewhere.

Backlinks, a.k.a. Textlinks

For direct traffic purposes, backlinks are fairly weak. However, as we will cover in greater detail in the next chapter, *links are a critical component to your SEO (search engine optimization) efforts.* There are numerous strategies for building links: they can be traded, purchased on a permanent basis, asked or bartered for, or leased on a monthly basis. The four most important criteria for gauging the value of a link are:

- The **relevance** and trust of the source website and page your link is posted on
- The **anchor text** of the link – the actual text that serves as the hyperlink to your site
- The **destination page** on your site the link is directed to
- The **type** of backlink (i.e. directory, article, press release, etc.)

Online Directories

Online directories are sites that list businesses and websites like the white and yellow pages of old. In some cases, and depending upon your market, they can successfully drive traffic to your site. For manufacturers and industrial suppliers, Thomas Net, the replacement of the print version of the Thomas Register, is one example of a directory seen to generate direct traffic to advertisers' websites. In general, though, directory listings are better served for other purposes; namely, as part of a link-building strategy to support your SEO efforts. Directories provide an affordable venue for getting relevant links to your site.

Multimedia Distribution

Video and audio files, in the right places, can be very effective mediums for driving traffic to your site. This became especially true with Google's purchase of YouTube, and the launch of Yahoo's video platform. In order to continually improve the search results, all the search engines are integrating video files into the organic search result pages, known as a universal results page.

Additionally, millions of users go to 3rd party websites to watch video content for both entertainment as well as product research purposes, every day (is it any wonder YouTube exceeds 2 billion pageviews a day?). Podcasts for download, streaming content on your site and on YouTube, all make for an enhanced user experience that builds brand, drives traffic and improves your SEO efforts. Audio interviews also provide similar value, though they may not get as much exposure.

As with anything, *quality* is a key component to success. We all have high expectations on video and audio content, having grown up with television and radio. For example, it's not enough to just throw something together and publish it; your brand and corporate image are on the line here, so make it worth your viewer's while. On the flipside, most videos that exist online needn't be television quality.

Formatted correctly, multimedia should be considered a requirement for any serious online marketing campaign. Testimonials, messages from the CEO, How-To's, etcetera.

Article Distribution

Publishing valuable information online, through press releases and articles is a great way to drive traffic, boost your brand, establish your expertise in your vertical or market place, and positively drive your SEO. Outside of SEO itself, article distribution is perhaps the most effective online marketing strategy. There are thousands of information-based websites that are continually looking for good content to publish every day. A well-written article has the potential to get published on dozens or even hundreds of websites. Again, formatting is essential, as you will want to include keyword-driven textlinks embedded in the content that point to specific pages of your site that deal with that keyword subject matter. This is called 'Deep Linking' in the industry, which means obtaining links to the internal pages of your website, and not just the homepage.

You will hear us speak of this over and over again throughout the book, as it plays a defining role to every aspect of online marketing, and that is *Relevance.*

Affiliate Marketing

Affiliate Marketing can be an extremely effective method for expanding your sales and marketing network with minimal investment from the parent company. As a service, it allows just about anyone to expand their sales channels exponentially through a network of affiliates that earns money on a customizable commission basis for a Cost Per Action (CPA) event. As the provider, you have the ability to set the commission event and percentage as you wish. Keep in mind, of course, that the more attractive your offering is, the more affiliates you will gain. Here is a brief list of the types of CPA events a business can create through an Affiliate Marketing campaign manager:

- Percentage of Sale
- Lead Conversion

- Pay Per Click
- Anonymous Data Acquisition

As a marketing solution, Affiliate Marketing has exploded in the online environment due to the diffuse nature of the Internet. As we are all well aware, the web is so expansive that it is essentially impossible for any company, regardless of size, to directly manage campaigns across even a tiny percentage of the available opportunities. There are millions upon millions of websites, in dozens of languages that could display your ads, and there are hundreds of thousands of people online that could potentially act as your commission-only sales force.

There are dozens of Affiliate Marketing communities (bringing advertisers and publishers of web sites together) and affiliate management tools available that make it incredibly easy to integrate as a permanent addition to your marketing and sales channels. Google it.

Offline Marketing Integration

While not an internet marketing strategy in and of itself, the value of integrating your offline marketing strategies (i.e. traditional media ads, radio, TV, etc.) and tying those efforts back to your online efforts will provide enormous benefit to all your marketing efforts. Again, all campaigns must be held accountable to evaluate ROI. It is stunning to us how companies are willing to throw millions of dollars annually at campaigns that cannot be assessed. From our perspective, a benefit of an unstable economy is to shake out the rug and get rid of the lice (yuck). Getting rid of wasteful advertising will only benefit those who know what they are doing and drive agencies that don't know what they doing out of business. Unless, of course, they get artificially propped up by the *congresscritters*.

Trade Shows: If you frequent trade shows, be sure to make prominent mention of your website. Showcase it. You may also want to allow people to sign-up on the spot for product updates, newsletters, or event calendars on-site. Another tactic we'd recommend, if on-the-spot sign-ups won't work, is to have people sign up with their names and emails, to receive updates as well.

What better way to build a database of *targeted, potential consumers* is there? Everyone who signs up is, in one way or another, interested in hearing more from you.

Print and Display Media: Is the perfect opportunity not only to generate brick-and-mortar foot traffic, but online traffic as well. Always tie back these media to your online media, whether it is a specific landing page created specifically for promotion or a best-selling brand product, there's no sense in making people chase down your website.

If they have to search for you, the chances of a possible consumer finding your competitors is extremely high. And what once was a solid lead opportunity has now been put up for grabs.

Television and Radio: In recent years we've seen more and more companies supplementing these media with tiebacks to their online efforts. As with traditional print media, the same holds true for television and radio. Give your possible, future consumers multiple avenues to engage with you.

Search Engine Marketing

Search Engine Marketing (SEM) incorporates all aspects of building a web site's exposure in the search engines. This includes "Organic Ranking," "Pay-Per-Click" advertising, and social media marketing. Organic Ranking is achieved through Search Engine Optimization (SEO) to acquire natural positioning in the Search Engine Result Pages (SERP's). Pay-Per-Click (PPC) advertising refers to the 'sponsored-links' fields of the search pages, which enable anyone to purchase clicks and traffic, with front page ad exposure, for any keyword.

The 6 Primary Aspects of Search Engine Marketing:

- *Keyword Analysis*
- *Search Engine Optimization (SEO)*
- *Pay-Per-Click Advertising (PPC)*
- *Local vs. National Targeting*
- *Multimedia Distribution*
- *Web Analytics*

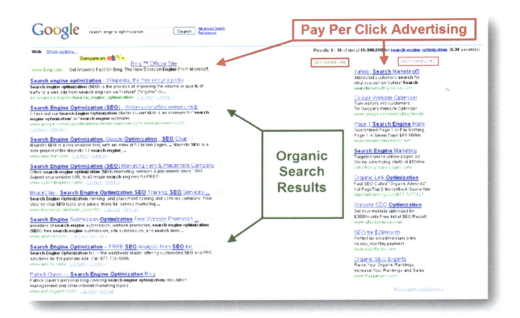

All the search engines follow similar strategies for ranking sites in the organic results, and all offer PPC advertising. **It is estimated that 80% or more of online queries and sales begin with one of the top 5 engines** *(Forrester Research, 2007).* Therefore, SEM is an absolute necessity for online marketing success and *should be afforded more importance and budget in the overall online marketing strategy, than all other forms of online advertising.*

Some 'cold hard' Search Stats:

- ***Search engines are the gateway for 80-90% of global user interaction with the web***
- Depending on your Target Demographic, Google is the solution for +60% of the market.

- Yahoo is currently managing to hold onto about 25%, while MSN's systems consistently fall under 10%.
- 'Eye Tracking' and Search Usability studies performed by MarketingSherpa®, indicate that approximately:
  - 80% of users find what they are searching for 'above the fold' of the very first page. In other words, in the top 5 organic or PPC results for any given search.
  - 90% of users rarely leave the first page of results, and less than 1-2% go beyond the second.
  - The top 3 organic positions receive the most attention

Moral of the story – **If your website is not displaying in the first two pages of search results, organically or through advertisements, you are virtually invisible to almost everyone online**. (And please, do not think you can make up the difference with Banner Advertising – It's not going to happen! A good banner ad, appropriately placed on the right website, will convert 1-2% of displays into traffic. As mentioned previously, banner ads are rarely effective for generating traffic.

Keyword Analysis

The backbone of any SEM campaign is the keyword analysis that allows an SEM professional to discover *exactly* what the public is searching for in relation to your product and service offerings. When we say "keyword," we also mean "key phrase" or "keyword phrase." For our purposes, they are fully interchangeable naming conventions of the same thing: the word, or string of words, entered into a search engine to find something online.

Search Engine Marketing constitutes what we like to call 'Reverse Marketing.' In the past, marketing was focused on 'pushing' the brand and product awareness out into the marketplace to create awareness, loyalty and sales. SEM requires the exact opposite. Traffic is 'pulled' in with enticements and relevant keyword matching, or "pull-marketing." *The process of keyword integration on your website encompasses many factors--most importantly the naming of your product according to the predetermined naming expectations of your audience.* For someone who is unaware of what a "Gizmo 2000" is, a savvy business owner must include the exact keyword driven name(s) of what that product is and/or does. It's about creating a convergence of brand and application.

Keyword preferences will change across geographical locations, genders, demographics, and are unique for all industry verticals. The keyword analysis is not just about uncovering words; it's a window into the mindset of your target audience and the public as a whole. It will provide invaluable guidance for establishing your company and brand online. Without this information, you have no rudder to steer an SEM campaign.

Keyword Analysis Tools

There are multiple keyword tools available that can be used to ferret out this information. In years past, a number of third party solutions popped up to fill the gap, like Trellian Keyword Discovery® and Wordtracker®. The main problem with all of these systems has been accuracy in traffic numbers. They each have their own scheme for projecting traffic amount per keyword, which are broad 'guess-timations' at best. Additionally, their keyword suggestions are just as inaccurate because they are based on false assumptions in the first place.

Finally, in 2007, Google began providing generalized traffic data in relation to PPC advertising, with fairly realistic numbers on ad display opportunities for AdWords' clients. It is called the Google Keyword Tool. However, their numbers are also skewed because they include their content network-- all the sites that use Google's AdSense system to display PPC ads on their site to earn a commission percentage of the PPC cost. That aside, this data is extremely beneficial for all SEM purposes because they provide an expanded list of synonymous keyword terms, the average PPC cost data, and global versus local traffic estimations. Additionally, as with majority of Google products, it's free.

The trick to properly using any keyword analysis data is to *avoid taking the stats at face value*. The numbers are not specific enough to make assumptions on the actual amount of traffic. How are they useful then? They are extremely useful in relation to each other. It is not necessarily important to know exactly how many people search per month for "shoes"; I guarantee there are a whole lot. What is useful is to know how many searched for "shoes," versus "sandals" or "tennis shoes" or "black leather dress shoes."

Picking the Right Keywords

Ultimately, the most important part of doing a thorough keyword analysis is that it enables us to choose the right words to target. The most common mistake people make is to assume that they should target all the keywords with the most amount of traffic. This may, or may not, be the case. As we will discuss more in depth later, your ability and the associated costs to rank organically, or purchase PPC traffic, for any given keyword is going to be entirely dependent upon the amount of competition. After more than 10 years of keyword research, we have yet to find a situation where multiple niche keywords were not available to be exploited by the savvy SEO specialist.

In other words, there are always 'hidden' keyword opportunities to target, that enable a business to affordably get in the game to obtain search visibility and traffic with relative ease. Therefore, picking the right keywords is the foundation of the SEM strategy that includes both short and long term objectives. The only limitation will be your budget.

Search Engine Optimization

SEO, again, is the implementation of keywords, content, and links to clearly define your products and services to search engines and users alike, in order to achieve top positions in the SERPS (search engine results pages). Keep in mind that you are dealing with an algorithm, a computer-driven mathematical equation, with set limitations and parameters of evaluation. There is nothing intuitive about it, with little to no comparative capabilities. In essence, this means that targeting "shoes" will not help your rankings for "sandals". Algorithms can make associations, but they are limited. Therefore, it is best to be decisive and clear about what you do.

There are numerous strategies to achieve top organic rankings, both 'good' and 'bad.' The bad SEO is referred to as 'Black Hat' and should be avoided at all costs; punishment is a one way ticket to the void-- your site will be removed from the search index entirely. We do not advocate, teach or use black hat practices. 'White Hat SEO' includes strategies deemed acceptable by the search engines and is based upon simple logic--what is good for the user is good for the search. Done correctly, SEO can provide the highest marketing ROI available today. However, putting keywords onto your site is just the beginning, and is generally not enough to drive a successful rank-building campaign. *There are dozens of alterations to be made for every page of a site, which often require ongoing refinement to improve results.* There are two primary aspects to SEO: Onsite and Offsite.

Onsite SEO

As the name implies, Onsite SEO is specifically concerned with the proper presentation of information, and the integration of keywords on a website. Simply put, search engines quantify a website's relevance and domain-level trust based upon what a particular website says about itself through content and internal anchor text (we are talking about onsite SEO only here). The search engines are directed to look at specific areas of a website to determine exactly what that site or particular page is about in order to define rank. An added bonus is that when done correctly, SEO will simultaneously improve your lead conversion ratios because your content becomes easier to digest for human users, follows a logical format (or argument), and is thus relevant to your target audience's needs. Keyword content considerations necessarily include:

- Heading Tags, Page Titles and Meta Data
- Site Platform and Coding concerns and requirements
- Content Visibility – just because you see it, does not mean the search engines can
- Site Navigation/Menu naming conventions
- Internal linking opportunities from every page
- Site Usability considerations
- Image naming conventions
- XML and HTML sitemaps

Offsite SEO

Offsite SEO is concerned with obtaining keyword optimized links to appropriate pages on the website. This is best summed up as what other websites across the web "say" about your website (now we are referring to offsite SEO). Links act as highly effective signals that attract the search engine's attention. Inbound links from trustworthy sites are used to both confirm what you are saying about yourself (with your onsite SEO efforts) and establish the *trustworthiness* and *relevance* of your webpage (website) content. Industry experts agree that offsite optimization is a critical component for successful SEM.

Offsite optimization is fueled by what are commonly referred to as "Backlinks". These are links obtainable from a variety of online sources, such as directory listings, press releases, blog posts, etc. Google revolutionized the search marketplace by including a website's interconnectedness to the rest of the web as a primary factor for determining rank. Therefore, your website's ranking is determined by the effective implementation of keywords both **on your site** and as **dispersed across the internet**. The object is to appear as a credible source of information and provider of your product and/or service, in relation to your keywords. In the industry, this is referred to as 'establishing authority.'

The search engines determine this through both the *quantity* and *quality* of inbound links to your site. *Quantity* is simply the number of links that point to your webpage or website as an authority--in most cases the more the better. *Quality* is a bit harder to define, as it is primarily a function of **relevance** and **importance**. Links from a site that is *relevant* to your industry will have a greater impact than one that is not. Furthermore, a link from an *important* website (as identified by Google Page Rank) will also maximize the impact.

Pay Per Click (PPC) Advertising

PPC (Google's "AdWords" and Yahoo's "Sponsored Search" systems, etc.) is the Search Engines' way of leveling the playing field and generating a sizeable income in the process. It is, in fact, Google's only sizeable source of income (other than maybe their financial investments). PPC lets anyone willing to purchase website traffic the opportunity to bid for keyword searches. The client gets the needed front-page exposure without the difficulties of SEO, and because of the bidding system, the market sets the value of that placement. Costs accrue on a per-click basis, as the name implies--not on a pay per display basis (CPM), as with banner ads.

One click through might cost the advertiser $0.10 or $30.00. It primarily depends on how much the competition is willing to spend. However, this does not mean you have to break the bank to get results. *The engines offer customizable restraints into the system so that daily spending limits can be set for each ad group and campaign, to fit any budget.* Keep in mind though, there are multiple other factors involved with how the search engines determine the cost of a click through, and having professional help is the key to maximizing your ROI. This is to say, *PPC success is NOT simply a matter of out-bidding the competition for a given phrase*.

The PPC cost per click (CPC) is also determined by the relevance of the target keywords, the ad copy and the content of the page the ad points to, known as **Quality Score** (a fairly new development within Google's PPC). This is particularly true with Google, whose revenue lifeline depends on their ability to provide the best results for searches. If they allow their SERPs to become cluttered with garbage, people will turn to another engine. To maintain their dominance in the search market by providing the best results, they have established a very effective system to weed out the chaff in the PPC market. Once again, it is a factor of relevance. Creating ad campaigns for keywords not directly reflected in the content of your website will exponentially increase your PPC costs. *Thus, SEO becomes increasingly important for your site as even basic onsite SEO will have a direct impact on your PPC campaign costs.*

Effective PPC Strategies:

- Only target keywords your website content can support
- Evaluate Position - while being in the first position can be important, it is often not cost effective. Additionally, lower positions *can* provide higher click-through-rates and better conversions – seems counter-intuitive, but it is true nonetheless
- Incorporate *Negative Keywords*: an extremely important filter for weeding out irrelevant traffic
- Focus on both the obvious and obscure keywords to find niche opportunities to:
  - drive quality traffic
  - minimize click through costs

An often-overlooked value of running a PPC campaign is that it can be the best approach for determining keyword effectiveness and ranking strategies for SEO. Knowing that "Manhattan Real Estate" is not the same as "Manhattan Townhomes for Sale," figuring out which is more relevant to your target audience, in addition to knowing which will be easier to target, can be of critical importance. PPC lets you find out within weeks what that difference will be, before committing to a long and expensive SEO process. Test the market with PPC before engaging in SEO. Within a few days, anyone can have a top-positioned marketing campaign underway.

Local versus National Search

An increasingly important function of SEM is the local versus national (or global) search opportunities available for businesses that service geo-specific areas. Local search is now integrated into PPC management systems so that businesses have the option to display their ads by zip code, state, region, country, internationally, and even to be mult lingual. With regards to SEO, integrating your geo keywords is critical if location matters. In most cases, it will be easier and more affordable to target your customers on a local basis.

Additionally, the major search engines provide opportunities to integrate your business location into their mapping tools. In the example below, you will see that the top section of the SERP is dominated by the map with 10 results that include name, website, and phone number. To ensure placement and the display or your correct information, you will need to login to each of the search engines and provide that data directly.

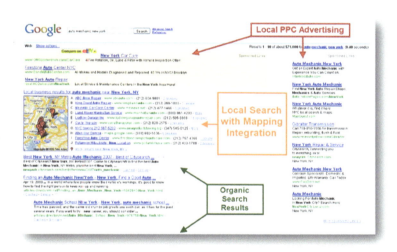

SEM Strategy

Site traffic from the search engines is critical, but traffic is only a servant to the Goal, and is not the Goal itself. Traffic is a "must have," but should not become the all-encompassing goal of a SEM strategy. All marketing campaigns, including SEO, exist to increase sales leads and profitability.

Traffic is a requirement to achieve this goal, thus SEO is enormously important. But keep in mind that your website must simultaneously meet the requirements for a multitude of equally important, co-existing strategies, which must function together to be effective. Arguably, the most important factor to marketing your company successfully online is the development of a strategy for presenting web content to the appropriate audience(s). Therefore, good SEO is not just about ranking for keywords; **it's the definition of online branding**.

Effective SEM strategies require:

- Extensive keyword research to:
    - Broadly uncover the range of keyword variations and opportunities in the marketplace in relation to your product
    - Narrow the results to the best keywords available to match your target audiences' expectations
- The integration of keywords into the appropriate places of your site for both search engines and various and distinct User Groups alike
    - Manipulation of existing content
    - Serves to improve content relevance in relation to your target audiences' searches
- Creation of new content and Landing Pages when needed
    - Expands the scope of available keywords to target
    - Landing pages are specialty webpages with targeted content for maximizing conversion ratios from both PPC and SEO traffic
- Various conversion opportunities to acquire leads and sales
    - Contact forms, Request For Quotes, etc
    - Downloads, PDFs, CADs, etc
    - Multimedia: videos, audio interviews, etc
    - Direct Sales events
- Analytics software to track all conversion activities to source and marketing campaign
- Integrated phone analytics to track calls generated from online marketing efforts
- The renaming of products, when possible, to match consumer expectations, which creates *Relevance*
- Information Architecture and Site Usability evaluations and improvements where necessary
- The integration of online and offline marketing efforts
- Ongoing evaluation and testing to continually improve the effectiveness of your strategies

How much should SEM cost?

The answer will always be a direct correlation to the amount of competition in your marketplace -- and your budget. The answer will also depend on the experience and skill of the SEM team you choose to involve. The general rule: the more experience and skill, the more the cost.

Like it or not, that is the determining factor for all forms of advertising. The more competing firms stand in your way, the more it's going to cost to dominate the engines for your keywords. Just keep in mind, the longer you wait, the more expensive it becomes. Every day, more companies are jumping into the game--and only the top 20 or so players, between natural and sponsored sections, are going to reap the benefits.

SEO vs PPC & PPC vs SEO

Advantages of SEO vs PPC:

- Organically ranked pages generally receive the highest click through ratios, averaging 5-10x more than PPC, depending on the market.
- As PageRank and the influence of SEO expand, a site's position in the search engine result page will appear higher, which increases legitimacy, increases trust afforded by the consumer, and boosts the appearance of expertise. SEO has long-term benefit.
- Once solid rankings have been established, the cost of maintaining or increasing that rank will be substantially less than a comparable PPC campaign.
- SEO, if done correctly, will simultaneously improve the user experience of your site. It will benefit your customers, because your content will be relevant to their search, efficiently cataloged, and easier to use.
- At this time, SEO has a direct impact on PPC costs by increasing keyword relevance, which serves to decrease costs through what is called a Quality Score'

Disadvantages of SEO vs PPC

- Patience is a factor! Building a strong search position for keywords is a slow process and requires dedication. It may take 2 months, or 2 years, *there is no way to exactly determine how long it will take to reach your ranking objectives.* It is dependent upon how aggressive you are, the skills of your SEO provider, and the amount of competition in your vertical or market place.
- Because it is a long term process, you will not see a great impact on your ROI in the short term. This does not mean it's not possible, but it is the exception rather than the rule.

Advantages of PPC vs SEO

- Immediate Results!
- Allows anyone to get top ranking exposure
- Customizable daily spending limits per keyword
- Real Time Tracking: Click Through/Spending Stats
- Fairly easy to use and control
- Allows user to set and compete for ur limited keyword fields
- Provides invaluable conversion feedback on keyword targets in real time

Disadvantages of PPC vs SEO

- Potentially expensive – just imagine a retailer paying $10 cash to everyone who walked into their store! PPC costs add up quickly, especially if you don't know how to effectively leverage your opportunities.
- Requires daily/weekly/monthly maintenance in most, if not all, cases
- Provides little long-term benefit to your site in terms of SEO efforts

As more and more people and companies are utilizing search engines as their primary shopping and purchasing medium, the Internet provides a business marketing cosmos unlike any other. Your product can be viewed by a larger audience than is afforded by any other form of advertising--an indisputable fact. *Therefore, it can be easily argued that a savvy business will dedicate the largest portion of its marketing budget to the internet, with the majority going to SEO and/or PPC campaigns.*

As with any marketing strategy, a sufficient budget is a must. The question is one of priority: **Immediate or long term results?** The best campaign will encompass both. A 50/50 approach is recommended, or something close to it; half to SEO, half to PPC. Utilizing this strategy, and assuming your budget is sufficient for your market, you are assured exposure and traffic now, and for the foreseeable future.

Another thing to keep in mind is that once organic ranking has been established, and the website/page is in the top 10 results for your keyword, the PPC budget for that keyword can be directed to new targets to expand your scope and exposure. Conversely, you can reduce or eliminate it if desired. However, as competition grows, continued vigilance will be required to ensure those hard won organic rankings are maintained, providing efficient ROI, and sufficient results. Many companies with top organic rankings are maintaining PPC advertising for the same keywords to guarantee top placement in both fields, for maximum exposure.

Tools of the SEM Trade

Google Systems

1. **Google Systems, in general**
   - All tools use the Google account user info, includes:
   - Google Docs – implementation tracking
   - Webmaster Tools – sitemap.xml file, search engine QA, detailed site CTRs
   - Google Analytics – primary analytics, included on all sites
   - AdWords – PPC accounts (limited accessibility)
   - URL Builder for campaign tracking in Google Analytics
   - http://www.google.com/support/googleanalytics/bin/answer.py?hl=en&answer=55578
2. **Google's Traffic Estimator – the AdWords Keyword Research Tool**
   - Designed for PPC, this tool can be used for SEO as well, to determine the most effective KW (Key Word) Targets
   - https://adwords.google.com/select/KeywordToolExternal
   - No credentials required

SEO Tools

1. **Wordtracker**
   - KW research tool
   - http://www.wordtracker.com
   - Subscription service requires purchase
2. **SEM Rush**
   - Expanded/long-tail KW ranking list
   - Paid Search Competitive Data
   - http://www.semrush.com/

- Subscription service requires purchase
3. **SEO Quake**
    - Provides a website evaluation tool set for backlinks, site, competitive evaluation tool
    - http://www.seoquake.com
    - Toolbar available for download and installation for your Browsers (preferably Firefox)
    - Only use as necessary – if it is left on, your IP will be blocked
4. **SEOmoz**
    - SEO community resource center
    - http://www.seomoz.org
    - Subscription service requires purchase
5. **Key Lime Tie**
    - Site scan system, sitemap.xml builder
    - http://keylimetie.com/Products/Sitemap-Generator/
    - Download and install program

Link Building Systems

1. **Link Diagnosis**
    - Link evaluation tool, can be used for your own site or others, to see all search registered Backlinks to any website you enter.
    - http://www.linkdiagnosis.com/
    - Download and Install browser plug-in, and begin your evaluation
2. **Directory Submission Package**
    - Affordable, mass directory submission package
    - http://www.best-web-directories.com/
    - Credentials – none, use the submission form
3. **PR Web**
    - Press Release syndication system
    - http://www.prweb.com
4. **Sponsored Reviews**
    - "Web Reviews" aka blog reviews, for link building
    - http://www.sponsoredreviews.com/
    - Subscription service requires purchase
    - An excellent suite of tools for managing many aspects of an SEM campaign, for yourself and for tracking your competitors, from one dashboard console
        i. KW Ranking reports
5. **Text Link Brokers**
    - A variety of link building opportunities from several link outlets
    - http://www.textlinkbrokers.com
    - Depending on services required; one-time fees and monthly, recurring fees

SEM Management Systems

1. **Web CEO**
    - http://www.webceo.com/
2. **Raven Tools**
    - http://raventools.com/
3. **Marin Software**
    - http://www.marinsoftware.com/

PPC Specific Tools

1. **SpyFu**
   - Deep competitive data on specific market place competition. International available. Subscription service, requires purchase
   - http://www.spyfu.com/
4. **Google's Web Optimizer**
   - Part of AdWords, this tool facilitates conversion rate improvement across unique landing pages or destination urls
   - http://websiteoptimizer.blogspot.com/
2. **Acquisio: Management Tool**
   - http://www.acquisio.com/
3. **Clix Marketing: Management Tool**
   - http://www.clixmarketing.com/

Chapter 4: Strategic Content Development

The eProfitability Wheel

I. **Defining the Layout - Information Architecture**
    a. IA Overview
    b. Structure & Designing with a Purpose
    c. User Path Optimization – aka "User Paths"

II. **Strategic Content Development Constraints**
    a. Constraints of the Search Engines
    b. Constraints of the Template – Standardized Layouts
    c. Constraints of the User – Learned Conventions

III. **Strategic Content Development**
    a. Create the Content for your Target Audience
    b. Content Layering

Defining the Layout - Information Architecture (IA)

IA Overview

What is Information Architecture (IA)? Information Architecture is the process web development companies use to create a "blueprint" for a website project. We say blueprint, as IA occurs prior to the website being "coded" and prior to the time design mock-ups (which agencies refer to as "concepts") are made. Information Architecture entails different things, depending on the web shop one works with. But in general, Information Architecture includes the following:

1 – Discovery:

Any website development shop worth its salt knows that each hour spent in *discovery* (and planning) saves multiple hours during the development phase. We always encourage, even for small website projects, that plenty of time be dedicated to discovery before one line of code is committed.

When we speak of discovery, we mean the process whereby an *Interactive* Project Manager asks a lot of questions, covering each detail relating to the project. For example: what is expected in terms of functionality, what was promised to the client, what was discussed between the client and the salesperson, and what was ultimately sold to the client, and making sure that all the necessary details are accounted for to ensure the project goes off without a hitch. It is impossible to produce a great product without "getting inside the head" of the client and "wrapping one's arms around" the site to be developed.

Again, any web development team that's on the level is going to be asking some fairly business-personal questions. Questions that probe to the heart of the business, not just what consumers see; questions that will make you explain the brand and what it stands for, how you're viewed in the marketplace currently, how you think you should be viewed in the marketplace, how your products and services are organized, and of these products and services; which are more central to your success (profitability). Once your team knows where you are, and where you want to be, they can begin to work on the site map.

2 – Site Map Development:

Once all the preliminary details are acquired, and the *Interactive* Project Manager has a handle on the entirety of the project at hand, a preliminary site map is generated. The site map will detail each page for a given site project and how each page relates (navigationally-speaking) to other site pages.

Site maps, as we've come to create them, typically look like flow-charts with the Homepage at the top of the tree and all sub-pages (Top Level Categories) and sub-sub-pages (Sub-Categories and Product Pages) extending from them with family tree-like relational lines. They should also include contact forms, privacy policies, about us page, and all other non-essential content pages. The industry calls these "Utility" pages. Unfortunately, these utility forms are sadly neglected as after-thoughts even though they are crucial to conversion success.

There are multiple tools to facilitate creating editable, useful website site maps:
- i. XMind
- ii. Microsoft Visio
- iii. TechSmith SnagIt

3 – Navigational Elements:

A good site map delineates a solid navigation scheme and vice versa. Often times, what separates a good site from a great site is how thoughtful the navigational elements are. These include the main navigation (or "main nav"), which is typically a horizontal row of top-level tabs situated between the header of a site (the top-most area) and a given page's "body" (in its broadest form, everything below the main navigation).

But when we speak of navigation elements, we mean far more than determining what tabs will comprise the main navigation. We also mean determining secondary navigations, sub-navigations, footer navigations, in-line navigations, etc. And not just for the public-facing pages either. Remember, in most cases, a website has two faces: the one seen by the general public and the one seen by administrators of a given site. A good site map will also help give your SEM team a head start in how they can start thinking about inter-linking website categories to create smooth indexing for search indexing spiders.

4 – Content Guide:

Although, the order of what is produced when can vary from shop to shop, in most cases a Content Guide is produced that adheres to the Site Map under consideration. By content, we mean everything from text and images to "rich media" (agency lingo for everything from video clips, to flash montages, to talking heads shot on blue-screen and overlaid onto a site, to slideshows, etc).

The Content Guide is crucial piece of the web development puzzle, as it normally entails assignments: who (which specified team member) is to supply or produce content that will live on the site when it goes live. In the case of catalog and e-Commerce sites, fulfilling the content necessary for go-live can be a serious undertaking; SKU numbers, product images, product specification, product values, parts numbers, schematics, downloads (such as PDFs or CAD files), and the like.

4 – Database Schematics:

If you ever dreamed of being a developer/programmer, we suggest that one day of database architecture planning should properly dissuade you of that dream! In most cases, creating database schematics is not a huge headache; in some cases such as the aforementioned product catalog-type scenario) it can be grueling.

Imagine a having to map the database elements and relationships necessary to sustain a 30,000-item parts catalog with online product "configurator" applications that enable visitors to customize parts and dynamically generate down-loadable CAD drawings in user-defined file types. We think Dante's *Inferno* only begins to approximate how much fun that might be. In any event, identifying the relational database structure is of course very crucial; it is a foundational piece of the blueprint developed during the Information Architecture phase.

5 – Wireframes:

"Wire-framing" entails creating very austere representation of specific pages or page-types (eg., a category page or product detail page). If we asked you to explain the layout of your current homepage on a piece of paper with a pen or pencil, it would likely look a great deal like a draft version of a homepage wireframe.

The value of wire-framing is the ability to visualize and begin to "lay out" (not in an artistic sense) where the page elements will be situated on a given page or page type on your site. We think it's unnecessary to wireframe each individual page envisioned for a particular site; however, it can be a very helpful exercise for the project lead, the project team, and the client alike. Not to mention, when done properly, the coders charged with developing the site are likely to buy you beer for having made their lives considerably more tolerable.

Keep in mind, Information Architecture is about discovering needs and wants and for solving issues. The real goal of IA is to sort out the production objectives *before* any significant programming has begun. Ultimately, teams that have a robust discovery phase generate excellent Information Architecture documentation (which culminates into an executable Project Plan)--saving lots of money, saving lots of time. Most importantly, a great discovery phase will save tons of headaches, heartaches, and stress on both sides of the table.

Imitation is the sincerest flattery. What are the successful sites that you enjoy using most? How can you adapt their layouts and features to best effect on your site?

6 – Interactive Prototypes:

An Interactive Prototype is just that: a prototype that simulates the navigational experience of the eventual website, including values in list boxes, labels for input boxes, image placeholders, etc. The intent is to let project stakeholders interact with the prototype in such a manner that they can anticipate how the eventual site or a specific piece of a site will eventually function.

In most cases, relating to your typical website development project, interactive prototypes are unnecessary (bordering on overkill). That being said, when a website project has many moving parts, incorporates a lot data, and is generally complex, and interactive prototype is indispensible. For example, if you had a small boutique with one store where used books are sold, an interactive prototype would be overkill (and somewhat expensive to have created).

On the other hand, if you wanted some way for users to buy, sell, preview, exchange books, browse new arrivals via video cameras on mechanical arms within the store, and enable folks to scan their favorite passages and upload them to the site, attaching to their user profile and favorite books list . . . well you get the idea: Lots of complex, moving parts. In this case, the project could benefit from creating an interactive prototype before actual programming begins.

There are multiple tools to facilitate creating useful website prototypes:
    i.   Axure
    ii.   Protoshare
    iii.   Mockingbird

7 – Project Plan:

The typical final product of thorough IA integrates all of the facets (1-6 above) of the Information Architecture exercise into a Project Plan or Development Plan. A solid Project Plan typically details production phases, dependencies, milestones, and action items (with attending dates and responsible parties) to some degree of the micro or macro (again, largely depending on the project and the best practices of the shop you are working with (and your budget).

In totality, then, it is this Project Plan and all of its appendices which comprise the "blueprint" of the website, portal, or tool to be built. If you prefer, it is a blueprint and a roadmap all in one. A reminder is in order here: different web development houses have different methodologies. In fact, different Interactive Project Managers (IPMs) usually have their own methodology. Some IPMs are more rote in their discovery. Others believe the best process is an organic process (re: SCRUM or Agile). Some live and die by what is and isn't in the contract, while some are more flexible, preferring to prescribe their own remedy, as long as it fits within the budget and time frame allotted them.

Some spend more time in discovery than others. Some ask more questions than others. Some are incredibly detail-oriented, while others are more intuitive. And they all have varying levels of experience. So, the thing to keep in mind is that sometimes you may end up with a very detailed Project Plan, as if written by an electrical engineer with too much time on his hands. On the other hand, you may receive a simple Gantt Chart with a list of action items and dates. Some IPMs may identify the "critical path." Some may not. Don't feel frustrated if the Discovery & Information Architecture Phase seems arduous. Don't feel cheated if it is painless. Don't feel ripped off if you don't get everything including an interactive prototype. If you have faith in the Project Lead and the team you hired, if you are a responsive client who makes decisions when asked, provides information and content in a timely fashion, and isn't given to blowing out the scope of the project at hand, the project will go more or less according to plan.

IA Process Resources:

For small websites, this will be a straightforward process. For bigger projects this can be a substantial undertaking. Regardless, it should be considered mission critical. Do not underestimate the importance of this step; its creation will literally save you dozens of hours in coding time, innumerable headaches and arguments (not to mention your sanity) through the development process.

Useful Resources for Information Architecture
i.   IAinstitute.org
ii. Information Architecture for the World Wide Web by Louis Rosenfeld & Peter Morville

Structure & Design with a Purpose

There is an inherent struggle in web design between those that would 'push the envelope' and those who stay with the 'tried and true.' The best is to find a happy medium, with a tendency towards the 'tried and true' side of the fence. All too often, especially in the agency world (a leftover from the creative drive of TV and radio), vendors will want something totally unique, rationalizing their *avant garde* (re: untested, unproven) suggestions as exciting and novel user experiences.

This has proven itself generally to be a great mistake, as we have seen time and time again in our experience. "Uniqueness" online is likely to produce confusion, misdirection, and abandonment of the brand. Creating a false excitement and all-sizzle web designs ≠ sales, revenue, or profitability!

As a book publisher, would you try to find new ways to print a book? Maybe mix up the chapters in a new and "exciting" order? Or print the text backwards so that readers have to use a mirror? No, obviously not, unless you goal is to destroy your author and your publishing company.

Then why do it online?

Performance is in consistency. Confusion is the enemy. Like it or not, user expectations have been set over the past decade and a half. It has been proven over and over again that users want websites to function like a phone book--obvious, simple, and easy to use. Users *will* respond to pretty pictures and stylish designs, as long as the rest of the site meets your users' inherent expectations (learned behaviors and otherwise). Overly complicated websites confuse users and chase them away. The opposite can be true as well: it is possible to bore your audience to death, drubbing them with stale design elements and useless information. You don't need to "reinvent the wheel"--all you need to do is make your site work for you! Remember, your website is *your company's face to the world*, and in many cases your site is solely responsible for creating that ever-important "first impression."

What does all this mean? It means stick to the standards, or if you prefer "Keep It Simple, Stupid."

Speaking of the KISS approach to web development, we should mention Steve Krug's **Don't Make Me Think**. It is an incredible resource for anyone interested in website best practices. Distilled to its most basic premise, Krug's book argues that web users will quickly abandon a site that is confusing or difficult to use. He rightly states that it is essential that everything of import be immediately accessible to the site visitor, and that the very best sites are *obvious* and *self-explanatory*. In short, if someone has to think, either to figure out where the information they need is hiding or to understand what you are trying to sell, they will abandon your site. This is not conjecture. Have you visited a government-run site recently? What is your first impulse? Likely, your first impulse is to turn and run away. Good thing the government has no competition! Just 'keep it simple' and you will have far greater success than most of your competitors.

- Site Usability Optimization – aka "User Paths"
    1. The purpose of the IA is not just to map content, it is to map your information in order to meet clear objectives. Again, keeping the Goal in mind, your website does not exist to educate the public, or provide pretty pictures, unless of course you have a Wikipedia model. Its sole purpose is to generate revenue and improve profitability.
    2. Enter "User Path Optimization". *UPO is the process of integrating your conversion objectives into the layout of the site*. This is not just including your conversion opportunities in the sitemap – *this is the process of building your entire site structure around the conversion events*.
        - Every page, every click, should be integrated with the intention of converting the user into a lead or a sale

User Path Optimization (UPO)

What are User Paths? User Paths are well-defined funnels on your site that guide users through the content of your site to predefined conversion goals, or "murder holes"--where visitors are converted into leads.

What is User Path Optimization (UPO)? UPO is the process of integrating your conversion objectives into every aspect of the Project Lifecycle: from discovery to information architecture. From the final Project Plan through the website development phase, quality assurance (QA) testing, and deployment phases. *Without keeping the Goal in mind, you might forget it altogether. Keeping the profit motive in the forefront of your mind is the surest way to do what is best for your business.* The Goal tells us that everything--including developing, maintaining, and/or improving your website--is and should be about profitability. *Without being user path optimized, we guarantee your site will not be able to fulfill its potential*.

Again, the objective of your site has nothing to do with Information Architecture (that is, how best to assign and present information pertaining to your company, personnel, products and services using web technology). The objective of your site is to wrench as much profit out of the marketplace as is technologically possible (with due regard given to all laws and business ethics of course). This is not to say that traditional Information Architecture and the disciplines it comprises are not exceedingly important. They are. But Information Architecture and the disciplines that comprise it are decidedly not the objective at all.

Hear us loud and clear: You can have an incredibly detailed, thorough, and even formidable Project Plan that everyone thinks is the be-all-end-all, with all manner of appendices and charts and tables and tech-speak. Congratulations (sarcasm intended)! Without keeping the Goal in the fore of your mind, all of the effort, while commendable, will amount to little more than a better-looking version of the online billboard you already have. That is to say, many a website has been "redesigned," "re-architected," "redeployed," and otherwise revamped without having done a damn thing to improve profitability. And in some extreme cases, by sheer negligence and shoddy craftsmanship, some "new and improved" portals actually have the absolute reverse effect of what was imagined . . . that of making a company's online presence even less profitable than it was before.

[Oh, and if you do deploy a new site, for God's sake make sure your vendor has all applicable "301s" in place. This is most important and oft overlooked, costing companies real visibility in the SERPs.]

User Path Optimization vs. Information Architecture

How does User Path Optimization differ from traditional Information Architecture (i.e. conducting discovery, creating site maps, wireframes, prototypes, content guides, and database schematics)? This is a messy question. Nonetheless, it is an important one to spend some time on. Traditional Information Architecture is oriented toward information (or content) and how best to display it (the user-facing website), store it (behind the scenes database stuff), and make sense of it (reporting mechanisms). In this sense, Information Architecture is aptly named. It is concerned primarily with (you guessed it) information. Moreover, Information Architecture lays the foundation for search marketing efforts going forward.

UPO, on the other hand, is squarely focused on maximizing Lead Capture and Lead Conversion (sales) ratios. That is, moving users through the site to the desired transaction (lead submission and/or sales conversion) as efficiently as possible.

As such, User Path Optimization puts the Goal front and center at all times--dictating that all aspects of the information architecture serve to promote the Goal. The short answer is that User Path Optimization (UPO) is a more appropriate form of information architecture toward the end of eProfitability--one that approaches information architecture in a more profit-focused manner.

UPO is about building your entire site structure and content around desired conversion events. When determining the information presented on your site, and its structure, it is absolutely critical to define it within the scope of Lead Maximization. That is, providing the easiest path to the point of lead capture as is possible. Every page, every click, should be integrated with the intention of converting the user into a lead (capturing the lead) in order to *convert* the lead into a sale. In the eCommerce setting, capturing the lead and converting the lead can occur simultaneously.

User Path Optimization – Rules to Follow

Orientation: *Where am I? What does this company do? How do I use this thing?*

Like being dropped from the heavens onto an alien landscape, the first thing any visitor to any site wants to know is if they've arrived at the right place. They want to confirm that your company does and/or sells that thing they're looking for. At the same time, synapses are firing behind the scenes either confirming the site is easy to use or informing them that the brain is likely to be overwhelmed by trying to figure it out.

Proposition: *What's the value proposition here – what's in it for me?*

Yep. Once the user is convinced he/she is in the right place, it is time to shake your tail feathers. Time to impress the object of your affections with your value proposition--state what they stand to gain from considering you above anyone else.

Suggestion: Next Steps / Calls-to-Action - *What am I supposed to do now?*

A site has mere seconds to engage a visitor, and this is no exaggeration. Now, if your site does its job, properly orienting the visitor and clearly stating your value proposition, you will have increased the likelihood of having an opportunity to induce the visitor to do what you want them to do. But this doesn't mean your work is done: far from it, in fact. What separates solid sites from excellent sites is *their ability to route visitors rapidly to the desired outcome*, and making transactions simple.   A huge part of that undertaking is making it abundantly clear to the visitor what it is they should do next.

Conversion

You've got their attention. You have them moving in the right direction. Now, like a jujitsu master, it is your job to use their own momentum in conjunction with your skills to convert the anonymous visitor into a lead. And, of course, there are many different ways to skin a cat, so to speak.

Applied User Path Optimization

Each site is different. As such, it is near impossible to say always do this, never do that. But there are some very basic best practices that all User Path Optimized sites employ to maximize their effectiveness. The following examples exemplify to ore extent or another, what makes a solid, effective, User Path-Optimized landing page.

B2BCFO – http://B2BCFO.com

The B2BCFO.com site is an excellent example of a site whose homepage is User Path Optimized. Within moments, a new visitor can answer the following properly:

1 – *Where the am I? What does this company do? How do I use this thing?* I am at B2BCFO.com, a site belonging to a company that is geared primarily to CEOs and Business Owners (the primary User Group or "audience"). The primary business this company appears to be in is related to securing cash and/or improving cash flow. The navigation appears very straightforward, very "user friendly."

2 – *What's the value proposition here? What's in it for me?* Well, let's see. There it is. If I self-identify as a member of the User Group "CEO or Business Owner," B2BCFO can help me with my cash flow (or get more cash), exit strategies, and fraud investigation. If I self-identify with the "CFO" User Group, I can learn more about joining (and the benefits of joining) the B2BCFO Team. If I am looking for "vetted" and "recommended" service providers, I can click to find those on this site too. This company also appears to offer books and a directory of in-network CFCs.

3 – *What am I supposed to do now?*   Again, this appears to be obvious. But, depending on the User Group I lump myself in with, I click on the appropriate "Click Here" button.

Analysis: Overall, this is an exemplary homepage. The only area we would suggest could use some additional work (in terms of clarity) is the bucket entitled "Service Providers." At first blush, we were not able to discern whether this section was for "Service Providers" as a distinct User Group or for "CEOs or Business Owners" looking to locate approved service providers.

LinkedIn.com – http://LinkedIn.com

A first time visitor to LinkedIn.com would have a hard time becoming confused as to what the site proposes and what the visitor is to do next. Pure perfection, really.

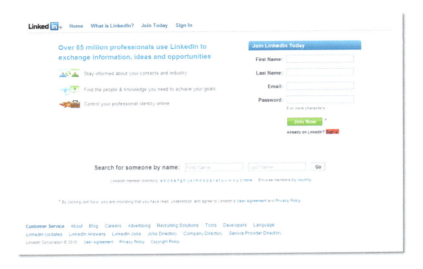

User Path Optimization – Things to Avoid

Speaking specifically in relation to User Path Optimization, let's evaluate the following sites.

Park Bank - http://parkbankplace.com

Yes. This is an unfortunate hangover from the late-90s. What in the world would possess a company--of all things, a financial institution--to have a "splash page" as the homepage of their site?

One does not know. So, don't do this to people. Also, we're not sure what the "Great Tree" refers to. Beyond just confusing the user with mysterious slogans, unless you happen to be a global Fortune 500 company, this is sure-fire way to severely hamper your search marketing efforts. Home pages are, in the overall majority, the most powerful webpage on a given site. Splash pages do not let that power, or trust, find its way down to other important pages on the website.

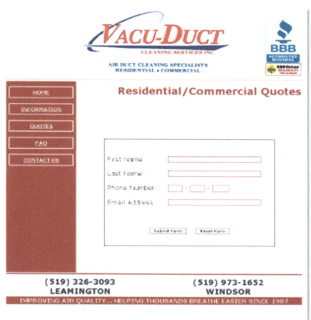

Vacu-Duct Cleaning Services Inc. – http://www.vacu-duct.com

Vacu-Duct Cleaning Services, Inc. presents another lackluster site. In this case, the only calls to action are buried beneath the fold (two phone numbers for two distinct offices).

These phone numbers and locations should be moved to the top. Additional investigation of the existing site reveals a "quote" form.

But you should notice something a bit more disheartening than the fact that the site expects visitors to click through to a form with no real value proposition: namely, this company provides "Residential" and "Commercial" services. But the homepage is geared near entirely to the "residential" user group. So, what is someone belonging to the "looking for Commercial duct-cleaning services" user group likely to do? We can guess.

We could not discern why the "request a quote" form was buried on a sub-page and not integrated into the homepage. The following is a quick representation of how modest modifications can yield significant results (assuming, of course, there is some volume of traffic to the site to begin with).

Young & Rubicam - http://www.yr.com

At the other extreme is the following example of company that seems to believe aesthetic is the be-all, end-all; these are the worst. And, for some reason, they all seem to be ad agencies. We are guessing they are living the "Image is everything," rock star lifestyle. Clearly, the absence of budget limitations does not translate into well-designed websites. That is all we can say about Young & Rubicam's site.

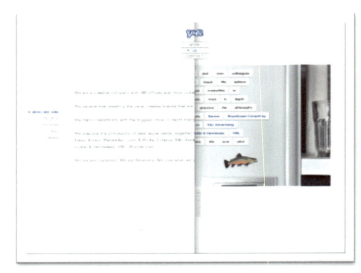

It may be that old media agencies really are so flush with cash that they can afford to be all sizzle and no steak. Alternatively, it may be that there is some currency in egoism in the business they are in. But for most businesses, this type of silliness is imprudent and best left to the "visionaries" of the world.

Conversion Events

Simply put, the conversion event is the point in the user's experience where your hard work pays off. You've optimized the architecture, the user path, have search engine optimized pages, and now you have the user right where you want them: on the edge of reaching out to you for more information, requesting a quote for services, or purchasing a cart-full of products. It's do-or-die time for your site. Everything you've done up to this point is in preparation for this single event: the sale.

Clearly, there is not a single site on the planet that can, or will, convert 100% of the users. Unfortunately, life gets in the way of that. However, if your site is only converting 1% of the all visitors on the website, then there's a little more than life stopping your users from converting. This would be a great time to look at your conversion event process.

Chances are you've never tried to buy anything from your own site, and you most certainly have never needed to contact someone in the company through one of your website forms. Well, now you get to. You should go through these forms as user and make sure the conversion event is as painless and efficient as possible. See the [**Forms Optimization**] Section for greater detail and explanation.

Strategic Content Development Constraints

Search Engines function through web-bots, or ' spiders," which are algorithmic-based complex data evaluation programs that build Search Engine Results Pages (SERPs) based on statistical analysis. Like mechanized armies of grand robot librarians, their job is to thoroughly catalog online information for the purpose of displaying highly-relevant and trustworthy results for any keyword search query performed through their sites. Google bots index information for Google. MSN bots for MSN (Bing), Yahoo! Bots for Yahoo!, and so on.

Search engines can only evaluate the content of your site based upon their limited quantification functions. They are not intelligent beings in and of themselves, and have no intuitive skills, like humans do (mostly), to connect disparate data sets that use variable linguistic descriptors (a.k.a. keywords). In addition, they can only make evaluations based on what, where, and how information is presented to them in the form of words: what words are used, where they are located, and how they are presented within the coding of your website. They are limited in:

- Quality – spiders, unlike people, cannot perceive the "quality" of writing of a given text. They will simply know whether or not the keywords on the page match a given query. Meaning, that a spider will not care whether Ernest Hemingway or Sam your next door neighbor wrote your content
- Intent – spiders cannot surmise the intent of a user. Again, they can only interpret the text on the page in relation to a query.
- Accessibility – spiders cannot access/process all forms of web content (eg., Flash content, AJAX content, multiple parameters (?= / id=) within URL strings).

Search Engine Friendly (SEF) Coding: Rules to Follow

<u>HTML</u> - To maximize your search engine presence, *use standard HTML-based coding whenever possible.* The search engines have definitely made numerous indexing improvements in the past few years to handle content in variable formats (most recently, JavaScript). However, the preferred format, for SEO purposes, remains HTML.

With our cloaking device, searchers will never find us, sir! Don't worry!

<u>PDFs</u> – The "Big Three" search engines (Google, Yahoo, and Bing) can and do index text-based PDF files in the search engine results pages (Google Docs even does optical character recognition on PDF files). Think of PDFs as another form of HTML content and optimize it as you would any other page on the website. Additionally, as Adobe PDF software offers meta-data fields for the PDF document, be sure to fill these fields out before creating the PDF to post on your website. Finally, do not use Photoshop or other image

creation/manipulation software. This will create, essentially, one large image of your content, which cannot be crawled by spiders. Use Microsoft Word or other word processing software to create the PDF content.

Non- SEF Coding: Things to Avoid

The stories we could tell about expensive, good-looking sites that ended up being coded in such a way as to be invisible to the search engines would make a good book. Suffice to say, your development team, from designers to coders need to understand how to build with search engines in mind. Unless of course you prefer to have a site with a Romulan Cloaking Device on it.

JavaScript – Please see Google's guide to writing SEF-friendly JavaScript: http://code.google.com/p/soc/wiki/JavascriptStyleGuide

JQUERY – You don't have to avoid JQUERY all together (in fact it's nearly impossible to avoid it these days), but again it's important to make sure you have a coder that understands the implications of using it with regard to SEO.

Flash - Agency folks love the multimedia presentation options afforded by Flash. Flash does make great presentations and promo pieces, but not easily searchable websites (unless specific steps are taken to make is "legible" to the search engine spiders. The single most important factor in good web design is accessibility, not glitter. Moreover, Apple has moved from Flash to HTML 5.

Constraints of the Template - Standardized Layouts

The following information is presented in a list format for quick reading. We don't want to get bogged down in the details, as this section alone could take a book in itself to thoroughly discuss. Nonetheless, it is crucial to familiarize yourself with following, as it should arm you with enough best practices to tell a well-crafted site from a poorly designed one.

Miscellaneous - Rules to Follow

- .com, .org, .net Extensions
- Concise URLs
- SEF URLs
- K.I.S.S.

- Clear Appeals to Primary Audience(s)
- Clear User Paths/Calls to Action
- Smiling People (women and men

Miscellaneous – Things to Avoid

- Frames
- Scrolling Tickers (Marquis)
- Terrible Color Schemes
- Animated GIFs
- "Glamorshot" images from the 80s
- Too Many Icons
- Misuse of Borders
- Really long links
- JavaScript Errors
- Giant Images
- Vanity Flash Intros
- Colloquialisms
- Poor Grammar/Typos/Bro en Image Links
- Too Many Fonts/Exotic Fonts/Too Many Colors

- Too Large/Too Small Typeface
- Width of Page Induces Scroll Bars
- Dead Links/Missing Pages
- Pop-Up Ads
- Auto-translators
- Keyword Cramming/Stuffing in the footer
- No skip button on flash
- No mute option on audio
- Local Weather plug-ins
- Multiple versions of site
- .info, .us, .tv, etc Extensions

Navigation Menus - Rules to Follow

Corporate Info Links (eg., About Us, Contact Us, Testimonials, Careers, etc) – Typically, these are incorporated in the far upper right corner of the header. These should be simple, discreet links, separated in some way. We like using a "pipe delimiter" |, such as seen in the image here:

Primary (Main) Navigation - These "links/buttons" represent your *primary user paths* and should provide direct access to all top-level categories. Primary Navigation elements, whether displayed horizontally across the top of the site and/or to the left of the body content, should be grouped so as to be an easily understood hierarchy of all categories and sub-categories. *Essentially, the main navigation should put "everything" at the user's "fingertips."*

Accordion-Styled Navigation – These work like, well, accordions. On-click or hover over a top-level category, and the navigation expands to reveal sub-categories. These are most effective when applied to larger sites, as they expand/contract on-demand (on-click), displaying subcategories as needed while saving room for the category currently being accessed.

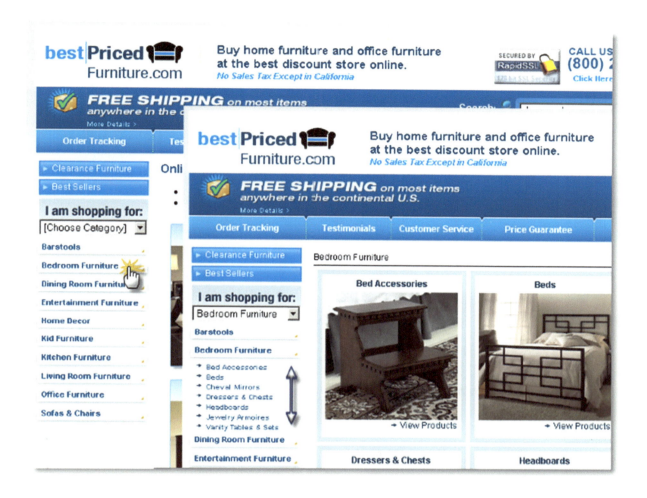

Footer (Bottom) Navigation – Footer navigations can include all corporate info links, but this is not the norm. We prefer to use this section to link to the privacy statement, site map, and terms of service. As for the type of separation elements used in footer navigation, we recommend simple, text-based, discreet links, separated by a pipe delimiter (example below), as we would use in the header.

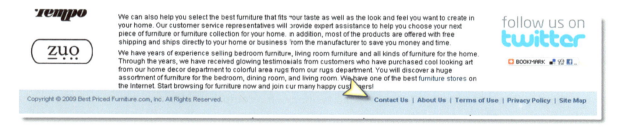

Onsite Search – Most users are accustomed to seeing the internal site search located in the upper-right as well, but at the edge of the header and below the corporate information links. On-site search is a very useful tool for both user and web owner alike. For the user, it provides immediate access to the specific content they are looking for (assuming it has been set up correctly/effectively to find all your content). For website owners, it provides invaluable stats on what users are looking for when they actually engage with the site. It's always a great thing to know what keyword from PPC or the SERPs drove them to the site in the first place, but learning how they interact with the site provides an entirely new level of knowledge.

Logins – this is going to depend primarily on the objective of the website. If the objective is to have people login to access content or use applications, then this may be a very prominent fixture in the header section of the website. In general the placement is for a logins is near/around the header region.

Navigation Menus – Things to Avoid

Convoluted Menus – Mixing different types of navigation into one; keep navigation types separate.

Right-Aligned Menus - Most people don't even look on the right side, as it is usually the most popular placement of banner ads. Avoid using if possible.

Flash or Image-Only driven Elements – As we've stated in previous sections, these types of elements (in general) cannot be easily indexed by search engines. CSS (cascading style sheets) in conjunction with JavaScript is extremely versatile and can make the links in the menu crawl-able by search engines.

Tabs for the Primary Navigation – Tab-based menus usually require drop downs, which are confusing for users to navigate through.

Massive Corporate Logos - There is a bad tendency for companies that feel the need to call greater attention to their corporate image or logo, to create overly large headers. This is an unnecessary waste of space.

Body Content - Rules to Follow

First and foremost, if you can, seek out a web-savvy copywriter--preferably one with a few jobs under his/her belt. If that's not in the cards, or budget for you, then consider all the content you write, for each webpage, as you would an essay, structuring each page as if you are defending a thesis with points of explanatory argument.

- Page Headline: This is what the page is about, as a whole. This is your argument, and should be the <h1> tag for the page
- Major Supporting Arguments: These are points that support your page headline, and should be the <h2> tags for the page
- Minor Supporting Arguments: These are points which supplement/support the major supporting arguments, and should be the <h3> for the page

Do use **bold text**, *italics*, and bullet points. These are indications to both the users and the search engine spiders that the text deserves special consideration. However, use them sparingly within the text; too much and you lessen the value of those special mentions and risk hurting the user's eyes.

Do use hypertext links within the body content. Allow the users to move through the website freely, especially when the link you provide is a supplemental the subject. Moreover, this will "flatten" the architecture of the website for spiders; that s, it allows the spiders to find pages in the website without having to rely on the navigation. Additionally, hypertext links internally also clue in the spiders as to which pages are "important" on your website.

Body Content – Things to Avoid

- Too many typeface sizes
- Too many font colors
- Too many embedded links
- Absence of "space"
- Too many Elements
- Too much Text
- Mission Statements on Homepage

Constraints of the Users – Learned Conventions

Logos – Corporate logos should be situated in the upper left corner of the site's header. On-click, user should be directed to the homepage.

Primary Phone Number – If this applies to your business, it should be located in the upper right hand corner of the header area. If possible, attempt to display a local number, as this can help local search rankings.

Logins – Whether a link or actual username and password fields, login call-to-action or form should be situated in the upper-right hand region of the site.

Order of Main Nav Elements – Should be listed left-to-right and/or top-to-bottom, running most important to least important.

Strategic Content Development

Now the "fun" starts. We have finally reached the point where we move from the planning to the building phase, utilizing the information collected and defined so far.

Overview:

- Keywords
- Product Descriptions
- Target Audience
- Sales Process Map
- IA Sitemap
- Conversion Goals

Create the Content for your Target Audience

Time and again, we see sites with content and information that fails to define clearly the product/service offering(s) of the site *Publisher* (the company to whom the site belongs). We also encounter sites that seem to have been produced in a vacuum by developers who seem to have no idea who the primary audience(s) may be, and were probably never asked to consider.

[*Remember, a great coder may know very little of the intricacies of search marketing… because she doesn't have to know more than how not to hurt the search specialist's efforts. You wouldn't expect a search marketing specialist to be an incredible coder . . . would you? Good. Because it is a rare pro who is a master of both disciplines. So, don't assume anything.*]

This is not just a matter of identifying whether your site is a "b2c" vs. a "b2b" portal. An effective website needs to go much deeper than that. Promote your offerings through content as if your ideal lead were standing in front of you engaged in a face-to-face conversation. Speak directly to their wants, needs, and desires. Tell them how your solution is the best available and what differentiates your products/services from the next guy. In essence, you have to tell your users what makes you special.

The average attention span of a web user is mapped out in fractions of seconds. You literally have 1-2 seconds to capture their attention. After that, you have less than a minute to prove your point. Prove your point and you can now engage the user with details, if necessary, or go straight for the conversion. Keep it simple: Remember, the objective is to convert a visitor into a lead (in order to eventually close them), not to overwhelm them with every detail of everything you can/will do for them.

Use scan-reading formatting. Few people will actually read the content of a web page word for word. They will scan it, so be sure your text is scan-friendly: use heading tags to call features out to users, use bolded text and bullet points. The bottom line is to make your content consumable in easily digestible chunks.

Content Layering

Landing Pages: The first page of entry. Ideally these will be all the primary pages of your site, as they will either be ranked organically for their keywords and acquiring direct traffic. These include:

- Homepage
- Top Level Category pages
- Landing pages created specifically for PPC campaigns and special offers

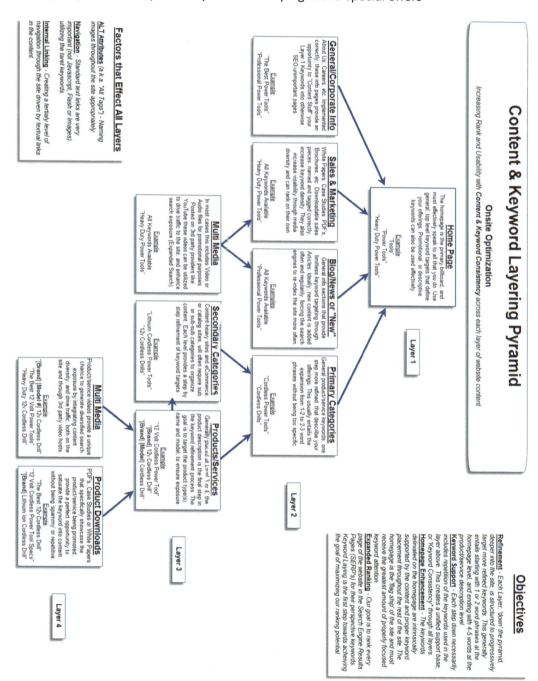

Chapter 5: Lead Capture

The eProfitability Wheel

Lead Capture Optimization (LCO)

Lead Capture and The Goal

Up to this point, everything we have detailed is the groundwork for the lead capture event. As we have discussed *ad nauseam*, the Goal is maximizing profit. Lead Capture (form inquiry, call, email, online chat, eNewsletter sign-up, or any other contact instigated by visitor to the site) is the defining process that enables the sale to become a possibility. Lead capture (and, of course, eCommerce sales) thus becomes an unequivocal standard to evaluate the success of your website and marketing efforts. With the exception of a direct e-Commerce system, lead capture is ultimately the goal of your marketing efforts: your website and all the campaigns combined. In the next chapter, we will provide very useful insight into how to effectively deal with Internet leads, but the purpose of this book is not to train or manage your sales team. Our focus is to get them the leads they need to close the sales ; it's up to them to make that transition from a lead to a sale.

How is lead captured? Essentially, there are two possibilities: through a form or a phone call. A phone call is self explanatory; there are, however, many different kinds of forms. When most people think of a website form, they inevitably think of their "Contact Us" page. As we have mentioned, these are necessary, but are perhaps the least effective method, at least in a traditional sense. We say this because *your typical contact us page is not user friendly*, asks far too many questions, and is ineffectual at traffic conversion.

Now that we have some background in what it takes to create an effective online presence, we can begin to appreciate that there are many different user types that will come to your site. Each of them is looking for something different. Additionally, the same person may come back to your site throughout the research process and each time be looking for different information based upon what stage of the purchase process they are in. From a practical standpoint, this means that your ability to capture leads and have an impressive traffic conversion ratio will depend upon your ability to meet their needs and expectations expeditiously.

This is the essence of the book, "Don't Make Me Think," where it has been definitively proven that the equation we are presenting here works. If you confuse the audience, they are left with a bad impression of your company and will not provide their contact info, unless they are desperate or have no other options. This is a sorry state to leave your potential clients in. Your website is your corporate brand, its face to the entire world, and it is critical to utilize all the strategies we have presented in order to drive conversions.

It is a simple fact that most of your visitors will never contact you. That's not the problem; the problem is when the structure, calls-to-action, presentation of offerings, design and/or your inability to effectively communicate with your anonymous traffic prevents you from making sales with people who are ready to buy. In other words, when visitors leave your site unimpressed and go to the competition because of a negative first impression/confusion/dissatisfaction, perception is more influential than fact. Regardless of the state of your company, you are evaluated by your ability to communicate. We mention all of this again, because Lead Capture is not about a form or a phone number; it's about communication, about setting the table for a conversation. The eProfitability cycle is a map to build effective online communication.

Forms *do* play an essential role in the traffic to lead conversion process. Brand and self-promotion is what gets your audience interested in you as a company. Your forms are what facilitate their impulse to communicate with you directly. Depending upon your product, there are many ways to enhance this channel between audience and provider. The more you can do to facilitate this bridge, the more people will use it.

We all have been trained by the Internet to expect ***instant gratification***. This includes the lead communication event. The single biggest mistake online, with regard to lead capture, is to ask for too much information upfront. Do *not* force your potential client to bear the burden of responsibility for effective communication.

For example, what's worse than calling a company, and having some degenerate, bored-out-of-their-mind operator pick up the phone, who proceeds to make you feel like a schmuck for even calling? Clearly, you are wasting their time, and consequently yours. We would propose that a poorly executed form is no different.

Therefore, if the sale of your product requires a phone conversation, why ask for more information than you need to initiate that phone call? All you need is a phone number and a name-- period. Not only is that effortless for the web user, it's easy for your sales team. It has been proven that on average less than 5% of general web traffic will click on a "contact us" page, and of that 5%, less than 5% will actually complete the form. There are two serious mistakes here:

- Why make someone click on a link to a contact us page in the first place?
- If everyone is abandoning your form before it's complete, you're asking for way too much information.

There are plenty of times that forms are required, just be sure you are using them effectively. Keep in mind that different forms should be used to target different user types. Up to this point, everything we have detailed is the groundwork for the lead capture event.

Various Types of Forms

1. Chat now/live chat
2. Quick Contact
3. RFQ
4. Contact Us
5. Blog/Comment
6. Feedback form
7. Surveys
8. Incentive based combo forms
9. Content download forms
10. RSS Feed sign-ups
11. Etc

In the final analysis, your lead capture ratio to traffic is the defining determinant of your online success, even if search engines don't take your lead capture ratio into consideration. If you have been effective, you will get leads, and hopefully see a double-digit increase from your previous baseline. If you are *not* getting leads, but have seen a significant increase in site traffic due to your marketing efforts, then something is most likely wrong with your presentation.

Forms Optimization – Converting Traffic

Everybody hates forms, but they are here to stay. That's a good thing too, as they are critical to your online success. You are permitted to continue to hate them, of course, whether you are a publisher or consumer, but you can't do without them. Forms are where buyers and sellers intersect online.   Forms represent the virtual version of a retail counter. Forms are where conversations are started, transactions are performed, and where deals are won or lost. Literally.

Take the following example: a consumer comes to your site, researches your offerings, finds what he/she is looking for, is ready to make a purchase today, clicks on "buy this item." If they become confused or overwhelmed (or both) by the form or process they are presented with, they're gone.

It might even be something that's absolutely critical to them, but they would rather not be bothered with figuring out what actions need to be taken to get that critical something. Another search, and they'll find someone else.

How about this one? Consumer comes to your site, likes what he/she sees and decides to contact your firm. The deal is in hand, but your contact us form is awful; requiring First Name, Last Name, City, State, Zip, email address, and Telephone Number, and, maybe, even requires they leave a comment of some kind. All they want to do is to establish contact with the appropriate party within your organization, and most likely they don't like being asked for so much personal data. In this case, you can blame spammers and scammers. They've made people gun-shy about giving too much information away, for fear that they'll be getting telemarketing calls, junk emails, and flyers to their home, just because they wanted to talk to someone at your firm.

These scenarios may seem far-fetched, but they are very common. In fact, we encounter awful (and sometimes downright criminally awful) forms nearly every day, even on websites for businesses that only exist online. Worse, you can find bad formson websites that web technology, marketing professionals, and executive-level professionals use: absolutely stunning and unforgivable. Some of the worst offenders are the larger, publicly-traded companies [read Fortune 500], whom one might think have the resources to see to this type of stuff.

When it comes to forms (whether simple or complex, whether one or multiple pages) if you don't optimize them, if you don't show them the love they deserve, you will suffer for your negligence. In virtually all cases, as we will see below, there is a significant improvement to be gained in this arena. We are confident that following the practices outlined below will afford instant benefits. So much so, that *if no other good comes of this book other than getting you to review and (if needed) optimize your forms, our mission to increase your web ROI will have succeeded*. If, on the other hand, you do everything we suggest in this book, yet fail to optimize your forms, you have only yourself to blame!

When it comes to optimizing forms, modest changes can yield an outsized benefit. Your online marketing efforts and website themselves really exist for no other reason than to get people to contact/converse/transact with you. No matter how excellent your pitch, no matter how beautifully convincing your online argument is, a crappy form can kill the deal in a heartbeat.

Forms – Rules to Follow

Of course, what people always ask us is this: "What are the best practices when it comes to forms?" And normally, web professionals like to say something safe like, "Well, it depends." And while it would be safer for us to say that, we aren't going to.

Audience Considerations: there is much to be said of considering one's intended audience (end user) when designing a form. We can imagine an unlimited amount of scenarios--for instance, language barriers, fluency, literacy, colloquialisms, the unintended consequences of choosing colors that carry negative connotations in a given foreign culture, numbers that may do the same, etc. So, yes, we agree that the end user for whom one form is intended is not the same as the end user for which another form is intended. We also agree that it is very important to consider these factors when building a form (or, for that matter an entire interactive marketing plan).

Contextual Considerations: Context is also an incredibly important aspect of designing an excellent form. For instance, if we already have the user's information on hand (i.e. the user is already logged into the website), it would be unnecessary to ask for parts of that information again.

Let's say a user wants to upgrade from a standard subscription (which they pay $5/month for) to the premium subscription (which costs them $20/month). Let's say they are already logged into their account when they decide to do so. Asking them for their email address and first name would be unnecessary and annoying, as we already have it on record. Asking them to verify their password before processing their order would be more tolerable, as the user would understand it as an additional layer of security. The point is this, the number of contexts within which forms are used is nearly infinite--as distinct as audiences can be from one site to the next.

Considerations for Learned Conventions – These are very, very important. Sometimes learned conventions are counter-intuitive. Sometimes they are relics from the dawn of the Internet. And sometimes they just don't make any sense whatsoever to those of us who work in the web sphere. Nonetheless, learned conventions are what they are. And there is no use fighting them. The simple fact is that it behooves us to put each element of each form in precisely the place the user expects it, because we don't want the user to have to give a moment's pause for any reason whatsoever. So, don't fight learned conventions, even if you are tempted to.

Even with all of these considerations, the "what-if" scenarios, the infinite variability in audiences, and infinitely variable contexts, we can nonetheless provide some safe Best Practices which when applied will help you to avoid common pitfalls we find day in and day out. Are these hard, fast rules that can be applied across the board with reckless abandon? No, they are not. Do they apply to 99% of all forms found online (at least relating to languages read left-to-right, top-to-bottom)? Yes, they do.

	Best	Better than Acceptable	Acceptable	Not acceptable
Label Placement	Above the Field	Right-aligned with Field	Left-Aligned in column	Below or to the right of field
Label Color	Black	Other	Other	Red
Label Font Size	14	12	10	<10
Required Field Notation	Asterisk – Red, to the right of Label, but to the left of field	Asterisk to the right of field	Exclamation point or color-coded field by default	Other
Examples of expected input	Below the field in smaller font size than label and italicized or embedded in the input field	Following label in same row, in parentheses and in smaller font size than label size	To the right of field	A legend
Help	Use only when absolutely necessary. And if used, use a "?" icon to the right of the field.	Use Sparingly		

	Best	Better than Acceptable	Acceptable	Not acceptable
Section Headers	When the form is "long" and the information being requested lends itself to being neatly partitioned	Even when form is not "long" per se, but the info being requested is more easily understood with partitions	Even short forms can be sectioned tastefully. Be careful of overkill.	Section header which is unnecessary, makes the form more confusing than it need be, or otherwise impedes the User from completing it
Steps/Subsequent Pages	When a form is in danger of being obscenely long. Or when it makes sense to capture one portion of user data before another set of data. When it is likely the user will not be able to complete the desired transaction in one sitting.	When failure to split the form into steps or pages causes people to run in the other direction.		Making people fill out a massive, never-ending form in one sitting. Or displaying a form that would reach to Shanghai if not for scrolling.
Progress Bars	Anytime there are multiple steps and/or subsequent form pages to be filled out, include Progress Bar or Step Chart.			Not giving the User visibility into how many steps/pages are required or remaining in the process.
Expectations	Always be honest about what the user's time commitment is likely to be when it comes to filling out a longer form or a process that includes multiple steps/pages. Additionally, never purposefully obscure the process or requirement. If the user needs to collect documents or information he/she is not likely to have on-hand, say so up front.			Understating the time required for the benefit promised. For instance, stating "Registration only takes 2 minutes!" when in fact said registration takes 15 minutes.\n\nMisleading the user – for instance, Intimating that a service is free – until the final page of a registration process.

Forms – Things to Avoid

computerjobs.com - form review

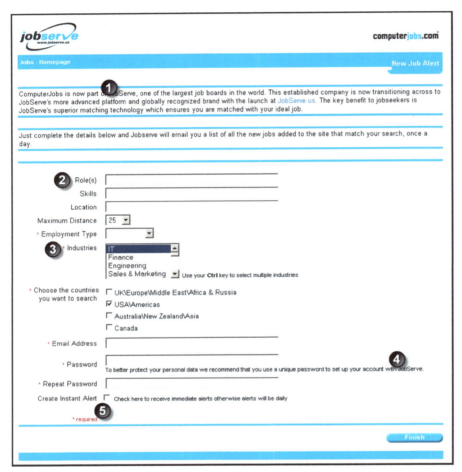

1 – **Too Much verbiage! Too much selling!** – Not only is a large amount of text copy off-putting (on a form in particular), the fact that the user has made it to this form indicates that the user has already been convinced of the benefits (unless he's writing a book having to do with Best Practices as it relates to web forms). In this case, the publisher seems hell-bent on continuing to pitch the service/product offered rather than "closing the deal." Forms are not the appropriate place to sell; they are the place to close!

2 – **Unfamiliar/Confusing Label** – You must put yourself in the shoes of the target audience. Look for constraints/obstacles that impede or cause the user to pause on a form. In this case, what is meant by "Role(s)?" Is it the Role I currently have? Or is it the Role I am looking to fill within an organization? Additionally, the (s) implies I should or might have several different Roles in mind (if I assume it is the Role I am looking to fill within an organization). What if I don't have more than one in mind? What do I do if I do, in fact, have several roles in mind? Am I supposed to separate each Role by a comma? In any event, making the user pause this early in a form is unforgivable. The first thing to do is clarify what is being asked. We would, in this case, recommend a label that reads "Desired Title" or something along those lines. Likewise, the "Location" label is equally bemusing. Is this the location the user is currently located in? Or is it the geographic location the user desires to eventually work in? If the latter, why is there no (s) added to the end of the label? Some clarification is in order here.

3 – **Labels in General**—It is desirable that they (again, in general) be right aligned to the input/select box. Additionally, in general, it is better to have the "*" or other character denoting "Required Field" come *after* the label.

4 – **Gratuitous "help" information** – In this case, the statement made below the "Password" input box should go without saying. That is, people understand why they are asked for a password. . . if not for security purposes, what in the world would a password be used for?

5 – **Asterisk Use**—This is a good use of defining what the asterisks stand for, but the "Finish" button should also be left-aligned and immediately below it. Instead, the architects of this form have placed it off to the right, below a horizontal rule. Additionally, while it may appear more aesthetically pleasing to demarcate the form labels in one column (white) and the remainder of the form in blue, it is needless. And, if it is needless, it should be removed. Remember, ask yourself "does this help, hinder, clarify or confuse? Is it useful or useless?" for each element on a given form. If the element is *not helpful*, *does not clarify*, or *is not useful*, remove it from the form.

Best Practices Applied

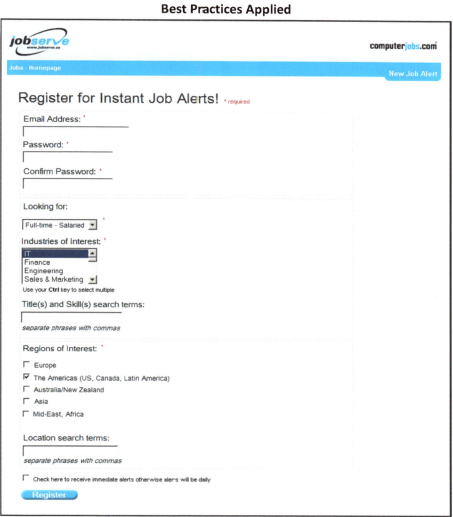

JustTechJobs.com – form review

1 - **Too Much verbiage! Too much selling!** – Again, the goal here is to close, not to sell. On the plus side, this form does have a page title (unlike the previous form we reviewed), confirming to the user that he/she is in the right place. "Register and Post Resume" is pretty straightforward and leaves little room for confusion.

2 – **Left-Alignment, Asterisks Risk, and Gaps!** - While having the labels left-aligned isn't the best way to go about formatting a form, it is acceptable nonetheless. The bigger problem here is having the asterisks to the left of the labels. It would be better to have them to the right of the labels themselves, not only because they cause the user to pause (which is a no-no), but also because when lined up as they are, they take precedence over the labels themselves. Worse yet, they make this involved form appear a bit more formidable (unpleasant) than need be. Another issue here is the space between the labels and their commensurate input boxes. Additional concerns: a) the colon following each label is unnecessary at best, and b) through the magic of web technology, the Zip Code field should be restricted to accept only 5 digits (thus making the 5 digit concern moot).

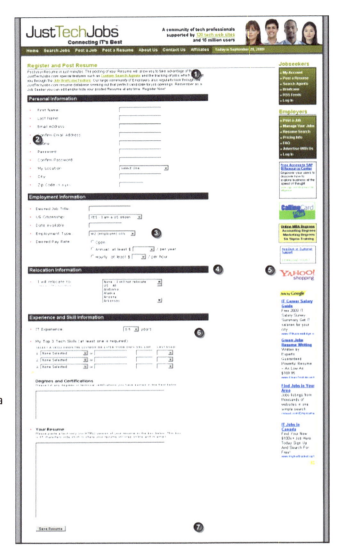

3 – **Terminology and Jargon** – The term "W2" is best reserved for HR professionals. One wonders what the point of including this level of detail is. Reviewing the values, one notes that the values "Employee" and "Contractor" and "Employee or Contractor" would remove the possibility of chasing someone away who might not know what a "W2" is.

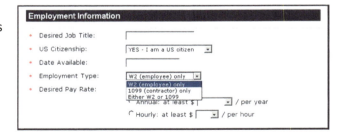

4 – **Nicely partitioned** – Given that this is a very long form, the architects of this form have made it less overwhelming by dividing the required information into reasonable sections with decent section headers.

5 – **Distractions** – The advertisements to the right of the form not only offer a distraction to the user, but also might actual result in users abandoning the process altogether. An apt anecdote here would be this: You've got your client signing the paperwork for a new car and on your desk you have brochures for competing brands. Not real smart.

6 – **Consider 2 steps instead of 1 huge form** – This form is mighty long. A good way to make the process less painful might be to split this process into 2 distinct pages, one for account creation and one for building resume details. In this manner, the account is created and the user can feel as if they've accomplished something concrete. Abandonment rates are likely to go way down, and the user can choose whether to continue completing his/her profile or to return at a later time to add work history details.

7 –**Action Button Use**—While the placement of the "Save Resume" button is excellent, we would suggest renaming the button to read "Post Resume" or "Create Account" instead. "Save Resume" is a bit passive and does not convey any degree of accomplishment.

Best Practices Applied

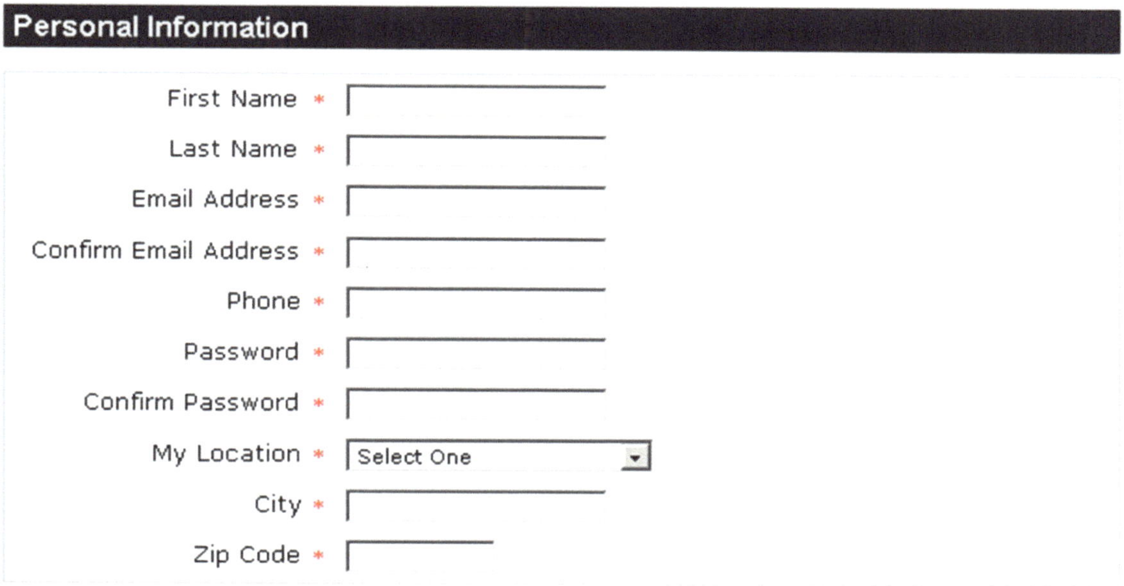

Personal Information

First Name *
Last Name *
Email Address *
Confirm Email Address *
Phone *
Password *
Confirm Password *
My Location * Select One
City *
Zip Code *

- *Labels have been right aligned*

- *Asterisks have been moved to the right of the labels*

- *Input fields have been moved in closer proximity to the labels*

- *(5 digit) has been removed*

Dice.com – form review

1 –**Land of Confusion** – "Step 1:" seems to indicate there are multiple steps. But if so, how many are there? Likewise, "Step 1: Create your account / login" intimates that there may be multiple steps to the process of logging in, which is not what we believe the publisher is trying at all to convey.

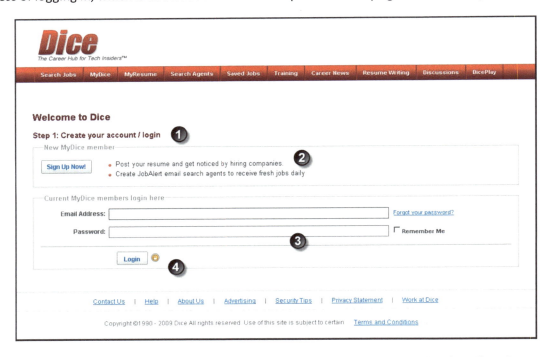

2 –**Form Explanation**—While the previous 2 examples we reviewed were absolutely guilty of overwhelming text and continuing to sell when the object by the time a user gets to the form is to close, Dice does a decent job of subtly reminding users what they are getting in return for signing up. Sure beats a paragraph (or two) of unwanted content. Nonetheless, we would recommend removing the bullet points entirely.

3 –**Field Length**—May be the longest input box we have ever seen . . . and that's *not* a good thing. While we are sure someone on the planet has an inordinately long email or some hieroglyphic password, we're not sure what the rationale at work here is. It sticks out like a sore thumb, so to speak, and in so doing is nothing but a distraction.

4 – **The Login button is fine as is for returning site subscribers**.

On-click of the Sign-Up Now! Button (which, by the way, was entirely missing from the homepage at the first pre-edited version of this book), the user is taken to the following form:

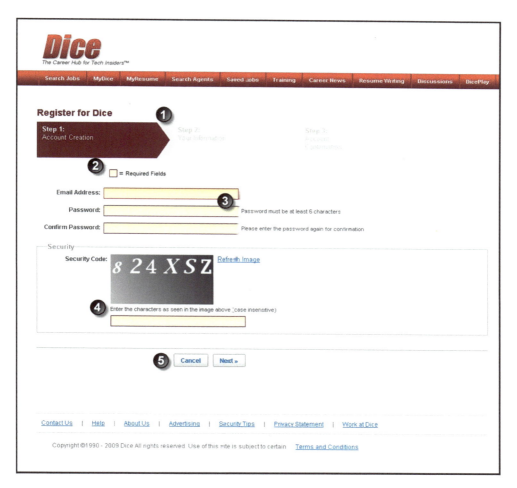

1 – **Setting Expectations Step-by-Step** - Here, Dice uses a nice 3-Step indicator, setting proper expectations for the user. In this case, Step 1 is highlighted in maroon, while the following steps (yet to be completed) are in grey. We might suggest also including something to the effect of "3 minutes to change your future" or "3 Easy Steps"

2 – **Is that a check box?** – The legend indicating that beige input boxes are required form elements looks at first glance to be a checkbox.

3 – **Gigantism** – Wow. Someone at Dice loves really long input boxes. Better to keep these more conventional. On the plus side, they do have their labels right-aligned.

4 – **Security? Really?** – This section has nothing to do with security. What it does relate to is making sure that people (not robots) are creating accounts. Better to call it what it is: "Human Verification"

5 – **Gratuitous use of Horizontal Rule**— Is only one nitpicky issue we have here. Also note that the "Cancel" button does nothing here but increase the likelihood that someone will inadvertently click it. Likewise, because it is to the left of the "Next >>" button, it appears pre-eminent. But we don't want people to cancel! We want them to complete the process of signing up. And finally, the Next button should be left aligned.

MilwaukeeJobs.com – form review

1 – Where to begin – It appears that this is a dual-purpose form: One purpose seems to be to serve as a login area for people with an existing account. However, it appears that the form is also for people who are looking to create a new account. In fact, we navigated to this page by clicking on a link that said "Register," only to find that we seem to have been routed to a form which assumes we already have an account (the page is entitled "Login to your MilwaukeeJobs.com Account").

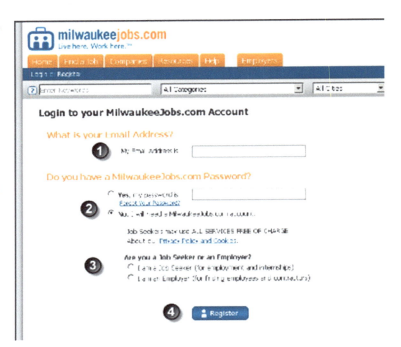

On the positive side, we are not offended by the conversationally (ad libbed?) styled "My Email Address is:" label, as it is clear and very much to the point. One may argue that it is redundant, however, as the label appears immediately below a section header which reads "What is your Email Address?" There truly is something to keeping it simple.

2 – More Problems – Again, because this form seems to be an attempt to merge two distinct forms (namely, Login and Create New Account functionalities), the form gets clunky here.

3 – Even More Problems – We stand corrected. This form is attempting to perform the function of 3 forms! Now, the user is being asked to delineate whether he/she is an employer or a "Job Seeker."

4 – Page Centered Form—The entire form (except, strangely enough, the two section titles in orange) is centered. Therefore, so is the "Register" button. Of course, we are best served not centering the form elements at all,

much less portions of the form elements. An additional annoyance is the icon to the left of the "Register" on the button itself. What purpose does it serve?

Here is what we would suggest with regard to this registration form:

Best Practices Applied

Are we serious? Well, only partially, because on further inspection, when we indicated for a second time that we were interested in registering for a new account (should never make the user ask twice, by the way) and clicked on the "Register" button, it turns out we hadn't registered at all. The registration process had just begun!

Before

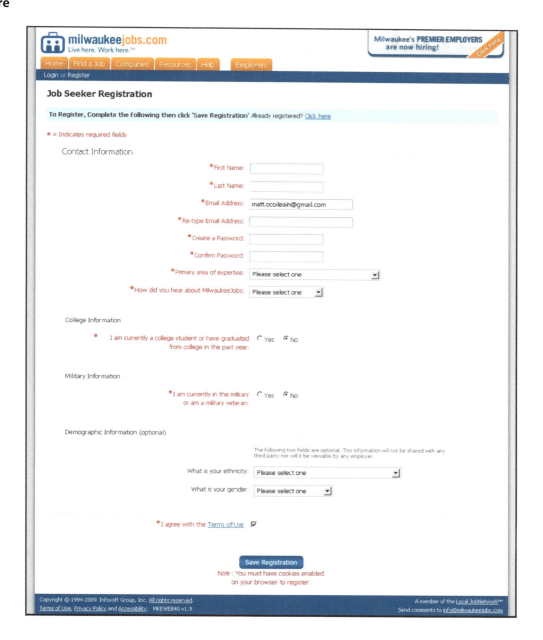

Best Practices Applied

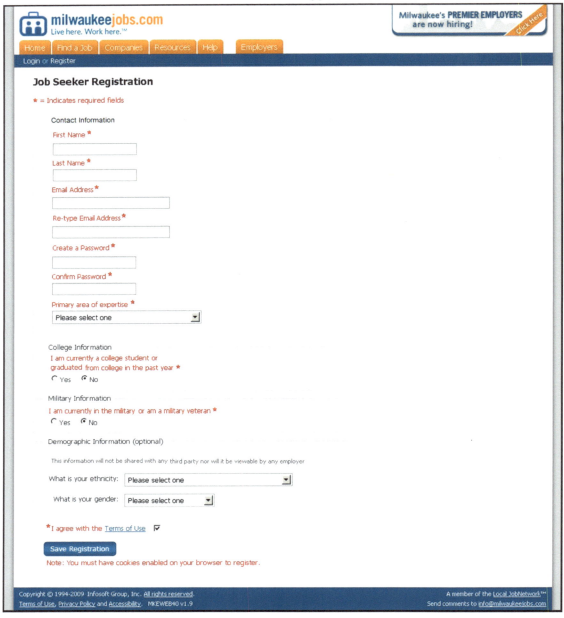

Wait just a second! Big word of caution: TOO MUCH RED is BAD! Better to make all of the text black……………………………………..

Best Practices Applied x2

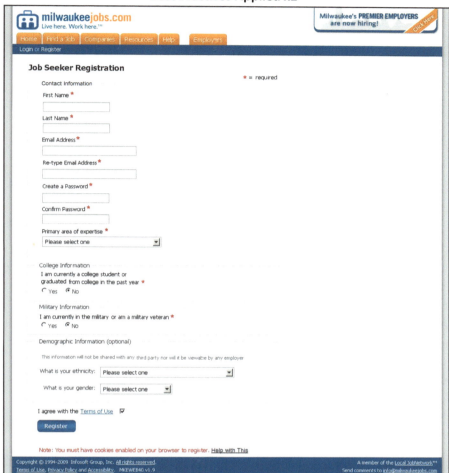

theladders.com – form review

1 – **Page Title Excellence** – This is the perfect use of a powerful call to action that seeks to set an expectation that the process of joining will take only 30 Seconds. For people making 100k plus, per annum, the marketing team for The Ladders seems to be applying the old adage "time is money" here. *But, does the process really take only 30 seconds? Or, will a User be asked for his/her credit card info on the subsequent page before his/her account is activated?*

2 – **Alignment and Font Size** - Again, the labels should be right-aligned. Oddly, there is an example of an email below the email label. Additionally, given that this site is geared toward an audience of high earning professionals, one can assume a high percentage of the users at this site are over the age of forty. Why is this significant? Well, the font size selected here is *way too small* for that target audience. It would be awful if users simply did not complete the form because of an inability to read the copy easily.

3 – "Retype" is a nice way of saying "Confirm" and possibly more accurate.

4 – Note that this form deduces your state from the Zip Code you provide! No need to ask for both.

5 – While we would prefer this form be in one column rather than two (the form is short enough that one column would suffice), we do appreciate that the architects of this form have opted for using radio buttons for both the "Select your field" section as well

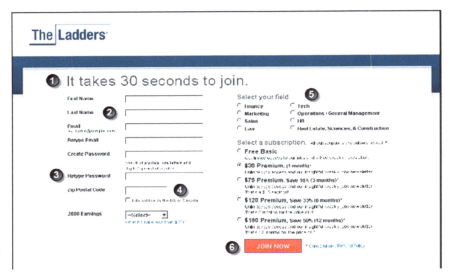

as the "Select a subscription" section. This is not to say that radio buttons are better or even preferred to select boxes at all. What we are saying here is that *it is always best to use the fewest number of different input types as is possible.*

6 – **The Red "JOIN NOW" button is overkill**. It's also in the wrong place (if you agree the form ought to be one column).

manpower.com – form review

1 – Excellent use of page title – this page title leaves no question as to what filling out this form promises the user.

2 – Excellent use of section headers/form partitions – This form's creators knew what they were doing with respect to partitioning the form in "bite-sized pieces." The section headers "Contact Information" and "My Manpower Account Credentials" are explicit. We would suggest changing the second section header to read "Account Credentials." Shorter is better in this regard.

3 – A couple problems appear with the input boxes on this form. While the form is otherwise very strong, we are not sold on the horizontal

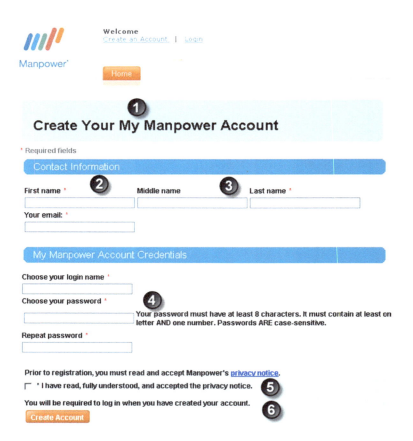

layout of the "First name," "Middle name" and "Last name" input boxes. If vertical length of the form were a concern, one could argue that laying these elements out in one row would make sense. However, given the short length of this particular form, we would urge stacking these elements vertically. An additional issue is the length of the "Middle name" field. We find it excessive. Also, it is unusual to ask a user for anything beyond a middle *initial*. Unless there is a strong case for asking for the entire middle name, we would suggest avoiding that. We do, however, applaud this form for not asking for an email confirmation. Most people these days are fairly adept at providing their email properly with one try. Additionally, most browsers are capable of auto-suggesting the proper values for many of these fields.

4 – While we appreciate the words of caution relating to choosing a password, we are not convinced that bold is the proper way to go. Likewise, the text is poorly formatted and there seems to be some issue with extra space between the label and the field itself.

5 – We would suggest having the privacy notice defaulted to checked. Having it unchecked, however, is probably a lawyer's suggestion. And we aren't attorneys. You should usually listen to your attorneys.

6 – Perfect button placement and message. The user knows exactly what to expect and what clicking on the button will do. Nice!

jobster.com - form review

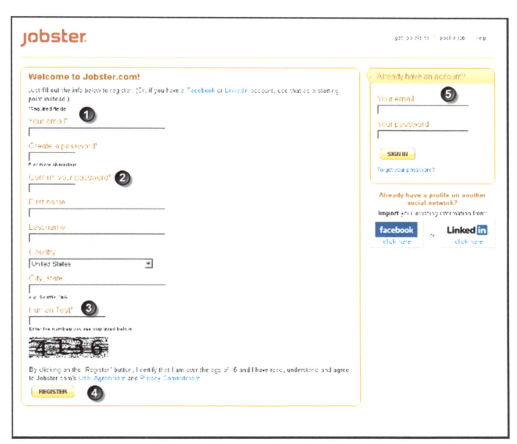

Now here is a form that applies all of the Best Practices in one.

1 - Perfect Label Placement – Above the input field.
2 – Perfect font size – Remember, not everyone can read 8 pt font. In fact, most people over the age of 40 can't do so easily.
3 – "Human Test" – calling a spade a spade, Human Test is what this is.
4 – "Register" button is perfectly placed.
5 – Unlike some of the other forms we have reviewed, this form's architect did not struggle with how to integrate a login area for users who already possess an account.

Whether you love or hate forms, optimizing a form (while not fun) is an easy place to start optimizing your lead-capture efforts.

Enticement Works

With a boatload of experience in web-based promotions, we can state unequivocally that enticements do work. If you prefer to call them "incentives" instead of "enticements," that's fine.

Of course, incentive-based lead capture is an art form unto itself. And while you may not be able to remember the last time you provided your email and name for a chance to win this or that, you've likely provided that exact same information for a free whitepaper, seminar, or a 30-day product trial . . . maybe something

as mundane as a motivational e-newsletter peppered with advertisements.

The point is this: people come in all flavors. While some drop their business cards into fishbowls every chance they get, knowing full well they are going to be marketed to, others cling to their email addresses as if a loved one's life depended on it. The majority of us fall somewhere in between. So, what is hokey to one person is irresistible to another person.

When done tastefully and in a compelling manner, very substantial gains can be made in boosting our lead capture ratios.

This homepage features four of the most basic calls to action: 1) phone, 2) live chat, 3) e-newsletter sign-up, and 4) directions. Even though these four should almost always be present on every single homepage in the Free World and beyond, most people would say, "Hey, other than the free newsletter, I don't see any sort of *quid pro quo* going on here." And we would say, "Well, we see the point you're trying to make, but we don't cede your point at all. Give it some thought. Why are these simple best practice inclusions on the homepage worthy of being called enticements (while only one can really be called "incentive-based"), as mild as we concede these enticements are? Give it some thought. It'll come to you."

Being tasteful is crucial. That is to say, the incentive (in the case of incentive-based lead capture) needs to be appealing, "of value," and plausible. Alternatively, the "hook" has to fit the overall context of the site, the business, the branding, et cetera. Most of us can cite instances of even the most conservative companies running seasonal promotions during the holidays. Because, in the context of the season, conservative brands can "push the envelope."

It goes without saying that certain industries, as off-color as they may be, are much more effective in terms of *enticing* transactions than others. One in particular comes to mind. But say what you will about that particular industry, theirs is one that is really at the leading edge of effective enticement, not just in the images they use, but in the mechanics employed as well. We'll leave the research to you, dear reader, as there is one industry that is nearly as good at lead capture enticement which does not involve such . . . erm . . .controversial content: namely, automotive (and in particular retail automotive). After retail automotive, we would suggest travel sites, Las Vegas hotels and casino sites. Also of note are those sites that sell virtual products, such as eBooks.

Here is an example from asamanthinketh.net that uses a "shadow-box" offer form. Hard to represent in text form, but when a visitor hits the site, the site fades and a this call-to-action enters the frame from the top. Hard to avoid this sort of pitch. And it is, regardless of what you might think, effective. Keep in mind that people aren't just stumbling onto this site. They are "in the market," searching the web for this sort of product. Of course, you'll immediately note that the offer is for something FREE. Presumably something of value. You'll also see that the publisher is only asking for First Name and Email. This publisher understands that enticing this information--

giving something "of value" in exchange for something (the most basic lead contact info) is crucial to establishing an conversation with his target consumer. He is growing his own home-spun email list, which likely has an open ratio of somewhere between 40-65% and per "eblast" an unsubscribe rate of under 3.5%. That is, each time he sends out an emailer to people whose info he has captured in this manner, some 45-60% actually open the email newsletter, while fewer than 3.5% choose to unsubscribe. Now that is profit-focused marketing.

[note: higher opt-out and bounce rates can be expected if the list owner abuses the list by sending too frequently, providing awful content, or using the list too infrequently]

Again, the key is to make sure that your incentive or enticement-based lead capture initiatives are proper, tasteful, and in context. For instance, the following example is one designed for a Harley Motorcycle Retailer. So, while it is appropriate for a motorcycle dealer, one can't imagine the same approach being appropriate for, say, a financial management firm or a doctor's office.

We liked this approach very much, as it had all the hallmarks of an highly-effective lead capture methodology. Again, it is hard to represent in text, but when a visitor comes to the site, a neat "transparent flash overlay" of a motorcycle comes from the center of the screen approaching the visitor, becoming "closer and closer" while dragging the promotional call-out (1). The promotional call-out is not too obnoxious, but it is impossible to avoid. Additionally, the enticement is appropriate and attractive. Who couldn't use 3 days and 3 nights in Vegas? Further, the promotion promises that "Every Player Wins a Prize." Of

course, the prizes are things like 10% off merchandise, 2 tickets to an entertainment event, and even a free oil change (which is interesting, as most Harley dealerships will do an oil change for free as a matter of course when a client purchases the oil at their location).

There are many forms out there for auto dealerships in particular which have simple forms into which you type your info and then print, and bring into the service department for service specials. What was neat about the example here is that it takes this process of lead capture a step further, including a cool flash game (2, a roulette game in this case. And the promise of every player winning a prize and the rest of the promo is included (3). Once the visitor supplies First Name, Zip, and Email, they click the Continue button. Upon so doing, the game advances a little further, the visitor is asked a couple multiple choice questions, clicks continue and the game progresses even further still-- until eventually the ball settles on a number and the outcome is presented in a printable form and an email to the same effect is sent to the dealer as well as the registrant. Very well-done.

We have all seen sites which have to take a more subtle approach to lead capture, such as exchange for a white paper, article(s), the ability to post comments, get coupons, et cetera.

The point is, it is imperative to do something. If you don't ask, you shouldn't expect to have much success. So whether you call it incentive-based or enticement-based lead capture doesn't matter. Just do something! A home-spun emailing list is immensely valuable, not to mention practically free to amass.

Chapter 6: Lead Conversion

The eProfitability Wheel

Defining Your Current Lead Conversion Process

Once you've identified who is responsible for fielding your leads and establishing the conversation with the prospect, the next step is to identify the rest of the process. In this respect, each organization is different, with different organizational structures, departments, personnel, needs, budgets, abilities, etc. In this respect, it is difficult to recommend too many specifics. Nonetheless, we can provide some generalities that will save you time and effort, from-experience and lessons-learned wisdom.

- **Document Current Lead Flow** – Whiteboard all incoming leads, first identifying all Lead Origins (not just from the website, but from all sources, phone, walk-ins, email, etc). Outline how all leads are fielded, to whom they are initially routed, assigned, and document the trail. If you use a CRM or Lead Management solutions (ACT, Salesforce.com, SugarCRM, homespun system), make sure to include the paths leads take within the system itself.

1. Phone inquiries – Are calls being logged? If they are sales inquiries are they just stuffed into vmail when no sales rep is available? Is any scrubbing being done to make sure the caller is being routed to the proper place?
2. General Vmail Boxes – Who is checking on these? Where are they being logged
3. Web Forms – identify all forms on your current site - check to see what email(s) these are currently routed to, respectively – you would be stunned to know how often our clients realize that the email addresses their forms are being shipped to no longer exist.
4. Non-personnel emails – for instance, info@yourdomain.com, sales@yourdomain.com – who is receiving those? What are they doing with them?

- **Mr. Yuck Exercise** – While on a job out in Denver, we were white-boarding a client's current lead management process, tracking down all lead sources, mapping all interactions between people and software solutions (such as ACT, disparate spreadsheets existing on this person's computer and that person's computer, etc.), following each lead path, 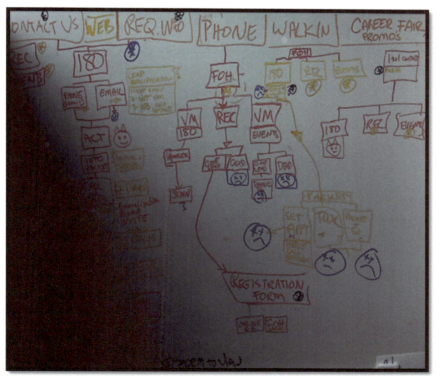 from inception to ongoing management. What we found was astounding: the amount of leads that lived and died in the System, having been ignored, allowed to rot, moved from spreadsheet to spreadsheet, and ultimately neglected in the long-run was simply amazing.

For each lead that followed some path that haphazardly led to someone who actually followed-up, there were 3 or 4 leads that didn't stand a chance at all. That is, there were process dead-ends everywhere, where personnel upstream had followed the loosely-identified and oft-illogical lead management "processes" only to be lost downstream. On the image of the white board, the frowns indicate lead path dead-ends. Totally unacceptable. Our dearly-departed James decided that this exercise of identifying failures and dead-ends in the current lead management processes, would forever be known as the Mr. Yuck Exercise. If you are unfamiliar with "Mr. Yuck," go ahead and Google him.

eLead Conversion Strategy Musts

Maximizing the sales conversion percentage of your existing stream of Internet leads should always be the *first step* in implementing a successful eLead Conversion Strategy.

Imagine your website as an online retail store or reception area. Treat your visitors in the same manner and with the same regard you would have for them if they came physically into your place of business, and you will do just fine.

Rapid Response – There is perhaps nothing as impactful as a rapid response to web inquires received through your site. Even today, we are stunned by companies (and their salespeople) who on the one hand complain about the difficult sales environment they face, yet on the other hand allow website leads to rot in their email for days and sometimes weeks on end. For instance, even those businesses that have benefitted immensely from the web sometimes do an appalling job of fielding web-borne leads. We are speaking specifically about real eEstate companies and their agents, as well as auto dealerships. It is far better to disallow visitors from submitting their contact info and questions than to ignore their inquiries. What does it say about an organization when a consumer goes to the trouble of contacting them only to be ignored? How likely is that consumer to interact with the organization again? Forward-thinking firms who are serious about the Goal respond within hours, rather than days or weeks. The best of them respond *within minutes*. Yes, we said minutes. Why is this so? Well, let's say a lead comes in via your website--it is a safe bet that person is shopping for a reason. They are not only primed, they are ready to start a conversation . . . and one presumably not having to do with the weather. If you want to really impress your prospective customers (or even existing ones), contact them immediately. The closer you can get to catching them while they are *still on your site*, the better.

So make sure you respond to all leads in a timely manner. This has to be an organizational expectation--if possible, a mandate. The more quickly you respond, the more likely you will be to convert your leads into sales. We encourage you to move incrementally towards the final goal. And in the case of lead follow-up, a solid goal is to eventually *follow-up with each and every lead within a maximum of 30 minutes*, even at peak times.

Always assume the prospect IS also shopping your competitors' sites. And always assume your competitors ARE following up with their Internet leads in a timely manner.

Thorough Follow-Up - Follow-up on the phone. If the prospect has submitted a phone number, they anticipate receiving a call-back. Auto-responders have their place, but quick-response follow-up phone calls increase sales conversion rates exponentially. If calling a prospect is not possible, a well-crafted, "personalized" email (that make clear to the prospect that their inquiry has been read by and responded to an actual human being) can be an effective fall-back. Nonetheless, email alone is NOT optimal. What you are looking to do is to establish a conversation with the prospect about what he/she is looking for. A timely phone call should be seen as a golden opportunity to increase market share. Nothing is more impressive to a prospect than receiving a phone call within minutes of an inquiry. This is especially true if you are in the service industry. Think about what it conveys. Do you let prospective clients spend more than an hour in voicemail ("voicejail")? Probably not. Do you let them wander around your place of business without trying to help them? Probably not.

FIFO vs LIFO - A very important point here is that there is a very strong positive correlation between time of inquiry, response, and the probability of consummating a sale. And while most professionals have an intuitive grasp that this is so, many are tempted to treat leads in a FIFO (first in first out) operational manner. On the one hand this makes sense: If one thinks of a line at a service counter, it would be disastrous to say, "Can I help the last person in line, please?" But let's say weeks have passed by since anyone checked your sales inbox. We would recommend attacking the most recent first. And this has everything to do with how "fresh" the lead is – because the "fresher" the lead, the more likely it is that a conversation will be established and a sale take place.

Responsibility & Accountability – Make sure all of the leads that originate from your site are sent to a responsible party that will treat each lead with the care, as well as the respect, each prospective customer deserves. Yes, it is commonplace for people to hate when additional responsibilities are assigned to them--or being held accountable for activities that were theirs to begin with but that they never before had to answer for. Nevertheless, it is crucial for someone or "someones" to "own" the leads that come through the web. Primarily, the reason has to do with making sure each lead is followed-up with in a rapid manner. Assigning ownership to someone, somewhere within the organization is a good first step. Without doing so, your leads will be lost in the haze of "other responsibilities" or treated like hot potatoes. And no one wins any deals with that sort of approach.

Round-Robin vs. Dedicated Lead Management – In high-volume and low-volume lead environments, the tendency is to default to a round-robin approach, assigning leads alternatively to Salesperson X, and then Salesperson Y, and so forth and so on. There is often enormous pressure to make sure salespeople are treated "fairly" in this respect. Even so, there are many reasons why the round-robin approach may not be the best approach to fielding leads. First and foremost, some salespeople are better than others. To make matters even more complicated, some average face-to-face salespeople do a brilliant job following up on eLeads, while some ace salespeople are terrible when it comes to fielding eLeads. Some can write well, while others cannot.

Some are lazier than others. Some have technophobia while others are technophiles. Some shop primarily online themselves, while others avoid the web like the plague. Point is, don't assume what you observe in your salespeople with traditional leads will translate verbatim as it relates to web prospects. And, in the end analysis, keeping the Goal front and center means that you want your best – and only your best – on each and every lead. Remember: the lead has provided their info. Moreover, they found you online and thought enough to inquire via your site.

But there is perhaps a more important thing to take into account when deciding whether a round-robin approach is the best approach, and this has primarily to do with learning curves. Specifically, if we assume two firms, one with a round-robin approach of 10 salespeople and one with a dedicated eLead Management professional. If we assume all 11 of them are identical in abilities and resources, the pay-off will be realized sooner by the firm with the dedicated eLead Management professional. The reason is that the dedicated eLead professional will be on a steeper learning curve, fielding more leads over X amount of time than any of the salespeople belonging to the group of 10. If, for instance, each firm is fielding the same amount of incoming leads, the eLead Pro will have 10 times the experience than any one of the 10 salespeople over the same span of time.

So, where possible, one person--or, depending on the size of the firm, one dedicated eLead Department--should be charged with first contact follow-up with all eLeads. Even if it is a matter of just scrubbing the leads as they come in, gleaning more information, setting an appointment for a salesperson, et cetera, *dedicated specialists are the best way to go*.

Quality Control - Use "secret-shopper" techniques to ensure that leads submitted via your site (whether sent to sales agents or to an Internet lead desk manager) are being handled quickly, thoroughly, and properly.

How to Verify Delivery of Submitted Consumer Information (lead flow) – This is a simple process to undertake. Pretend you are a visitor to your site. Fill out your forms, sign up for newsletters, request a quote (or whatever applies). S ee what transpires. Did you get a confirmation message that your inquiry has been sent? Did the confirmation message clearly state next steps or what the consumer can expect now that they have shown an interest? Did you receive an automated confirmation via email (auto-responder)? Did the auto-responder email make sense? Does it clearly state when someone will be following up with you? Did it include a link back to your site, a phone number, an address, special promotions, correct personnel information?

On the other side of the equation is whether or not the inquiry was routed to the appropriate party within your organization. To whom is it supposed to go? Is that person still with your company? Do you even know who is supposed to receive the leads or how the site is currently configured in terms of who or how notification takes place? If not, it is time to ask your web master or IT folks.

Chapter 7: Client Relationship Management (CRM)

The eProfitability Wheel

Reduce, Reuse, Recycle: There are very few things as valuable as a Lead database. Of course, your Client List may qualify as being more valuable. We'll give you that. But a lead database is up there. The two need to exist in the same place. We hard y need to explain why this is so, but we will anyway.

Existing Clients and Prospective Client Leads are the lifeblood of business. No matter where they originate, whether web, walk-in, phone call, whether referral or not, you must treat your Lead database (and, of course, Client database) as you treat your Client database.

It is vastly easier to upsell an existing Client than to convert a Prospective Client. And any sales pro will tell you that incoming unsolicited leads are preferable to cold-calling. The obvious reason is that unsolicited leads, even if driven by advertisirg, are easier to close than soft leads. But most sales pros are more concerned with today's leads, with closing today's deals--so focused on closing fresh leads that they forsake leads that hit the sales pipeline a couple weeks or months ago and weren't immediately closed. Granted, this has as much more to do with human nature and dollars and cents than any intent to neglect viable prospects. It's just easier to sell a Client than close a Prospect. And easier to close an unsolicited Prospect than drum up new leads.

Nevertheless, it is crucial for the organization to keep on top of all leads that failed to close immediately. The reason is obvious: Not al prospects are in the same place in the buy-cycle. Some are doing research as to who offers what in the marketplace. But these "window shoppers" aren't looking just for the sake of looking. And they certainly aren't instigating a conversation with you (in the form of a lead) for kicks. Sure, they may be 3, 6, 12 days/months/years until they are ready to make a purchase, but they *will* be making a purchase. And they can either buy from you or someone else.

Many organizations have strict disciplines in place with regard to "Client Touch-Cycles," the idea being, 1) to make sure your clients "feel the love," but also because, 2) the more love they feel the more they spend with an organization. Prospective clients are much the same. The more love they feel, the more likely they are to decide to become a Client. So ignoring these folks is stupid.

Touch-Cycles should be created that take prospects into account. The organization should be disciplined enough to be able to track and execute mid- to long-term relationship-building activities similar to disciplines in place for the organization's established clientele.

If you don't already have a CRM solution in place, you need one. There is no better time than the present to begin the process of putting one in place. There are no excuses left for not having one, and plenty of reasons to introduce one to your organization today. For most organizations, the price for a robust solution that meets the business's needs is minimal. And there are some very fine open-source solutions which are free. Here are a few suggestions:

- Salesforce.com
- ACT.com
- SugarCRM.com
- Microsoft Dynamics CRM

Whether you have a lead management (CRM) solution in place or not, invariably you've got a pile of leads here, a pile there, some from a convention in Vegas a couple years ago, others that have survived a couple sales managers, existing in 13 different format across 20 different spreadsheets, legacy systems, et cetera. Don't let this scare you away from determining to improve your organization's behavior and processes.

The first thing to do is identify where all Lead records presently exist. And once you've figured that out to the best of your ability, you're going to want to consolidate all of them in a central CRM solution. It's a pain well worth the effort. Again, it is unacceptable for anyone within the organization not to follow the rules with regard to Client records and Leads. Everyone must be committed to interacting with the central CRM solution--and also must agree to resist the lazy temptation to keep their "own list" using their "own lead tracking methodology."

It used to be the case that cost was the primary excuse for not implementing a CRM solution. And in the olden days, that was a serious consideration. Nowadays, most of the hesitation comes from internal resources that are suspicious of "new initiatives," especially those that might lead to heightened accountability. Then there are those who will gripe about the time and effort required to implement a CRM solution. For most organizations, though, this is an unwarranted concern. Things have changed drastically with regard to the CRM options in the marketplace. Unless yours is a truly unique organization that requires a truly custom solution, then today's CRM solutions will work just fine for your needs. We promise. T his is largely because the CRM Solutions Industry has matured significantly in the last 5 years. And today's solutions, while they can be customized to whatever degree you might think you need, are all "configurable" to such a degree that an out-of-the-box, standard install need only be configured for your specific needs.

The step after implementation and customization (configuration) is to train your crew and put in place rules of engagement for using the solution.

By the way, most CRM solutions include operations/production workflow modules, as well as proposal builders and the like. If you want to see what's happening now in the world of "CRM," check out Salesforce.com's Appexchange: absolutely amazing. Key takeaway is that "CRM" is not and should not be taken to mean solely "Customer Relationship Management" these days . . .because CRM is much, much more than that now.

As previously mentioned, the best organizations, regardless of industry or size, maintain their Client and Prospects databases in a centralized location, with clear ownership delineation, responsibilities, assignments, procedures to maintain an up-to-date contact database, and "Touch Plans" for records of each classification, category, and status.

Whether a simple Client Check-up (check in) by your Customer Service Manager, an Upsell Program targeting existing Clients who could benefit from a new service offering, or an eNewsletter, or a courtesy call to a prospect at 3-month intervals each contact in your CRM Solution, whether Client or Prospect, should be assigned to one or multiple distinct and complementary Touch Plans.

Again, we know it sounds daunting, and likely it will prove to be. But your competitors are doing this sort of stuff. And if they aren't, there's even more reason for your organization to be doing so. So no more excuses. It's time to get your s**t together. The idea is to sell more stuff. And a good first step is getting rid of excuses.

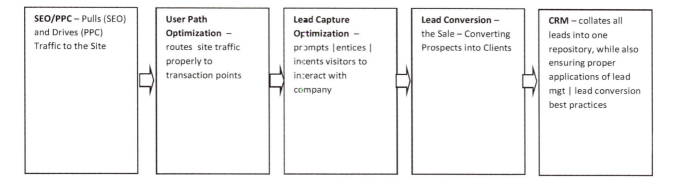

| SEO/PPC – Pulls (SEO) and Drives (PPC) Traffic to the Site | User Path Optimization – routes site traffic properly to transaction points | Lead Capture Optimization – prompts \|entices\| incents visitors to interact with company | Lead Conversion – the Sale – Converting Prospects into Clients | CRM – collates all leads into one repository, while also ensuring proper applications of lead mgt \| lead conversion best practices |

Chapter 8: Defining the NEW Sell

Your website is the cornerstone of your corporate brand. With the widespread acceptance of Web 2.0 standards of interaction and the professionals who have "grown up with the web" entering the managerial ranks, even the most cynical have come to accept that a website is not just a billboard. Your site is the foundation of your company's public presence (or should be), and you will be judged by it (whether you like to admit it or not). However, the point of this book is not to provide a "How to Build a Website" guide. There are plenty of resources available that go into much greater detail, especially on the implementation side.

Our objective is to provide a holistic philosophy and an in-depth appreciation for the interrelatedness of all aspects of the eProfitability Wheel. Our objective is to provide business decision-makers the framework for *building a holistic web presence: one which is informational, garners traffic, captures leads, advances the cause of converting leads into sales, resulting in profitability. **That** is the Goal of this book.* To accomplish maximum profitability requires an all-encompassing marketing and branding plan that serves as the foundation for all your company's marketing.

The eProfitability Model advocates a Holistic Approach to maximizing you Web Presence, because all aspects, whether Traffic, Content, Lead Capture, Lead Conversion, and CRM, are interpenetrating.

Starting from Scratch

While your website isn't the only consideration, it is a crucial to have an excellent one. Some of our readers may indeed have excellent websites. Others will have sites that are serviceable. But most of our readers have likely realized that their respective sites are less than adequate, and far from excellent. If you are among those whose site is severely lacking when taken as a whole, it will be easier to embark on a "redesign" (i.e. new site build) from scratch, rather than attempt to refurbish a tired old site. If this is not an option, the following information still holds true.

Whatever you are up against as it relates to proposing and getting authorization for a new site, or even trying to improve an existing outmoded lump of a site, organizational politics usually means that someone is going to have to navigate a no-man's-land of competing interest and egos.

Constraints of Competing Interests

Inevitably, one of the biggest challenges faced by business website owners, or managers, is the creation of a meaningful strategic plan for content development. Remember, when we speak about user groups, we are not speaking solely about extra-organizational groups. We need to consider internal user groups as well (sales, management, customer care, public relations, investor relations, business development, etc.). We need to consider the needs of all of these user groups. Developing content that meets all the potentially contradictory expectations is perhaps the most grueling challenge involved.

What are some of the most common competing interests and inherent tensions?

Consumer User Group(s) – In most cases, it would be complicated enough balancing the wants, needs, and desires of your various consumer audiences   Let's say you sell B2B and B2C. Let's say, further that with regard to B2B, you have different offerings for small, medium, and large concerns.

Internal User Groups – To complicate matters further, you have to consider internal User Groups, such as the Executive Team, the Legal Team, the Sales Team, the IT Staff, the Customer Service Team--each having very different visions of what the site should do and how it can (should) work to advance their respective goals. Satisfying these User Groups is perhaps the biggest challenge, as ego, organizational politics, and unrealistic expectations are nearly impossible to avoid, no matter how many appeals to "team spirit" you invoke.

In music circles, there is a saying that "everyone is a guitarist": invariably, after every show someone wants to talk to the lead guitarist about their own guitar-playing acumen. In the web, we have a similar saying: "Everyone is a web designer." The worst scenario for web vendors and internal project leads as well is a manager who believes he or she is an expert in the interactive disciplines . . . that is, unless they are demonstrably interactive experts.

Another admonishment is this: Nothing good can come from designing a site "by committee." This is one of the surest ways to get everyone's hackles up and accomplish next to nothing over a long period of time, while expending enormous amounts of everyone's time. So, "involving" people (or, rather, making them "feel" involved) is one thing. Empowering 13 people to veto this or that on a whim, interject this idea and that idea *ad nauseam* is suicidal. We would recommend that unless you have a limitless budget, you pick one point person, give them the task, work with them on the objectives, to the degree you feel you must. But use prudence.

If you trust the person assigned to the task, then it means you have faith in them, or at least enough faith to assign them the responsibility of executing such a potentially massive project. And if you are going to give them the responsibility, then you must give them the authority to make decisions. Your web vendor will thank you profusely. It is far preferable (and less-expensive) to have one point of contact.

Designed by Committee

One person who, yes, may have to report back to others and even take into account their recommendations, but ultimately one person who has authority to make decisions. Even the authority to make judgment calls, including this and excluding that. Trust us on this and you will be much happier for it. Sure, some feelings may be hurt along the way. But at least you'll retain your sanity.

And, if want to understand just how bad things can get, read Matthew Inman's How a Web Design Goes Straight to Hell.

Search Engines as a User Group – As the eProfitability Wheel dictates, no one aspect of the wheel can be considered without considering how it interrelates with the others. So, one cannot discuss tensions among User Groups without ensuring nothing is done to impede the desires of the Search Engines. Remember, the Search Engines are not human. They are algorithms. This means they are programmed to anticipate certain things on a well-constructed site. So, while it is weird perhaps to speak of them in terms of possessing human sensibilities, it is easiest to speak about them in these terms. Search Engines do have preferences, expectations, proclivities; their primary purpose is to discern the best results for specific searches.

We need to make a solid argument to them. Our job is to construct a site, structurally (Search Engine Friendly URLs, Taxonomy, Site Map, Robot txt files, 301s, etc.) as well as content-wise (text, multimedia, metadata, etc.) that the search engines find irresistible. Or, at least, relatively more attractive than any of your competitors' sites.

You can see why creating equilibrium where there is very little to be found among the common tensions and competing interests is no easy task. And we certainly understand this, having seen it play out first-hand too many times to count.

Is there an easy solution? No. There is no easy solution. Most businesses don't bother developing an effective method for solving it, either because it appears insurmountable or they don't even know they should solve for it. Given our orientation towards the Goal, we recognize working to establish some equilibrium among the competing interest groups is crucial to online success and efficiency. Ultimately, you will have to deal with these competing interests, ideally sooner rather than later. ***Doing it right the first time, while necessitating more work upfront, will save exponentially more***

work and money in the long run. Better to work it through now rather than attempting to do it after the fact.

Why is this so important? Because a clearly defined scope and focus for your website content, can be used to guide and structure the entire marketing direction of all on and offline marketing efforts. This is not to say that changes won't be made along the way. Nothing is perfect the first time around, nor should that be expected. Nor can you expect to fully account for everything you need beforehand. However, having a defined scope and strategy for your website is immensely powerful and will act as a unifying force across all your marketing initiatives.

The process begins with your website, and ends with the complete plan of your corporate marketing strategy--which is exactly the way it should be! In the Digital Age, it is your web presence that serves as your marketing foundation. Every campaign, from print to trade shows, SEM to Banner ads, should reference and reinforce your website.

Most large companies have agencies, or internal marketing teams, who are responsible for this seemingly formidable task. Small to mid-sized companies do not have such a luxury. We would argue that this is a good thing, an advantage to be exploited to its fullest. In the 'olden days,' large corporations were able to create monopolistic dominance in a marketplace controlled by television, radio and print media. Today the converse is true. As mentioned previously, traditional agencies and 'marketing experts' are struggling to understand the interactive experience, which sets up a perfect 'David and Goliath' scenario, where the underdog can effectively out-compete, and completely overwhelm the giants. They may have huge budgets, but they are rigid and change is a difficult thing to institute, and in most cases they are way behind the curve as it relates to the web. As a result, they are forced into reaction to the trends set by small, flexible companies. Having said that, they can afford to make mistakes that the small business cannot. This is why it is imperative to do everything you can to succeed, do it right the first time, and remain flexible.

For every hour spent in discovery, planning, and scoping out your new site, 3-5 will be saved in development hours. Again, you're going to have to trust us here. We know whereof we speak.

Why the Online Market Requires a Unique Approach

We have presented multiple reasons why the web is unique. Previously, it was up to the companies themselves, or their agencies, to push brand- and product-naming so heavily as to ingrain it into the mind of the masses. Print advertising, radio commercials, late night television spots, and even direct mailers were all designed to force feed the public regurgitated marketing claptrap. It was and is the essence of "Push" marketing.

> Online, this type of marketing is highly ineffectual.
> **Q: *Why?***
> **A: Unavoidably, we have a multifaceted response.**

First of all, the medium itself is not easily exploited by traditional advertising methods (Flashy ads, voice-overs, talking heads, and lame actors? Forget it). Secondly, the web is literally owned by the masses, it is the destroyer of corporate-owned network model. Finally, the Internet is an interactive tool, not a passive one. **Participation is a requirement**.

Tired of being blasted with endless, senseless advertisements from every direction, internet consumers:

- Ignore banner ads
- Avoid sites that spam them with obnoxious advertising
- Have the ability to navigate away in 'the blink of an eye'
- Are capable of finding a competitor in a matter of seconds

In other words, the web user is in control of the experience, from start to finish. Thus, we have the revolution in associative marketing techniques. While the end goal is the same, the rules have evolved, and the 'consumer' holds the cards. To be effective, your site, your content and your messaging must cater to the end user's wants, needs, and desires. End of story. Your job is to give it to them fast, direct and free (whenever possible).

An incredible facet of the online sell process is that the catering of content begins long before someone even comes to your site. How you define yourself with words, not pictures, will first determine whether you are even found, and secondly if someone will visit.

Q: *Where does first contact happen?*
A: **In the great majority of cases it's not a print, banner or video advertisement: Enter what we like to call the 'Search Engine Marketing Experience.'**

Search Engines are a powerful tool that, for the foreseeable future, are the essential interface for presenting and finding online content. At present, their dominance is absolute. Whether it's products, services, multimedia, or just information that you are marketing, get it in the search engines or your site will die in obscurity (unless of course you have hundreds of thousands to waste on 'brand building' the old way).

What are the apparent lessons?

- Your Product(s) must be named and defined within the scope of your target audience's expectations
- To successfully market yourself online , you have to be on the front page of the search results *for your relevant keywords*
- The search market becomes daily more competitive

Defining Your Product

The search engines provide a revolutionary approach to product naming and identification. Keywords are the singular words, or phrases, that people use to define the search.   Using the right tools to uncover the hidden treasures, it is fairly easy to find the primary keywords people are using to find your product(s).

Q: *Why is this important?*

A: Because the user defines the relationship.

SEM is what we like to call 'Reverse Marketing'. *The user defines what to name the things you sell.* Brand is no longer the defining quotient in relation to search; the 'key' words used to describe your product are. This is not to say that brand is irrelevant. Brand still has pull with consumers, and willfully ignoring that is just as dangerous as not targeting the keywords users use to search for your products and services. Ideally, you'd like to see a mix on the website of brand and user-defined keywords for a given product or service.

By determining what keywords the marketplace uses to name the product, you are accomplishing 2 of the 3 primary mission goals of strategic content development--matching both users' and search engines' expectations! Using keywords to define your product will permit search engines to find and digest your site and products easily. Additionally, those descriptions will match the user's predefined expectations of what they are seeking. This is called "relevance":

- Relevance to Search
- Relevance to the Audience
- Relevance to the Corporation

Striking this balance is the "key" to success   Obtaining relevance for all interested parties will exponentially improve your profile. Keep in mind that keywords alone are not enough--the keywords act as the guide for the development of all site content, when integrated holistically and to their maximum benefit.   This is true SEO, and could be considered the foundational online marketing strategy.

Keyword Research

The 'Key' to proper keyword identification falls, once again, on the strategy (right now we are speaking to the strategy of determining which keywords to pick, not how to implement on your site). The strategy for picking the right keywords will be an organic process with your website, as there will be a learning curve.

At this point, we only need to know the "primary" keywords (seed words), or the broad targets that will be used to define your whole site and ts primary content categories and sub-categories. In many cases these are self-apparent; in others they will not be. Regardless, doing your homework will have an enormous impact on every step of the content creation process.

As a synopsis, here are some rules of thumb:

- Try not target the most visible, highly-trafficked keywords
  - These are the 1-2 word keyword phrases
  - They are broad, general, and not likely to bring high-quality traffic
- Consider the options in relation to the specifics of your product categories and sub-categories
- Consider the options in relation to the expectations of Upper Management

In many cases you will find multiple variations surrounding a handful of primary identifiers, such as:

- Power Tools
- Electric Tools
- Electric Power Tools
- Portable Tools
- Cordless Tools
- Professional Power Tools

While every variation may fit from a product critique, from an effective SEO/SEM standpoint, we suggest finding mid-long-tail keywords (three and four phrase keywords) to use within top-level categories and sub-categories. Keep in mind, that each page on the website should be targeting unique keyword phrases that are **directly related to the content on the page, benefitting quality ratings.**

With a few hours of research on your own, or with the help of an SEO professional, you will have hundreds of relevant keywords to sift through and refine. Just keep the Goal in mind. To properly define your product for the web market means attracting consumers who are most likely to transact.

How to Do Initial Keyword Research:

1. **Pick your top 5 products/services, and find the 3-5 main ways of describing them.**
2. **Run each group through Google's Keyword tool**
3. **Evaluate keywords based on a KEI (keyword effectiveness index).**
   a. If using Google Keyword Tool (KWT), KEI can be evaluated through
      i. Average Cost Per Click: The more expensive a click is, the more likely that a keyword will produce conversions. Otherwise, no would pay for clicks at exorbitant prices.
      ii. Advertiser Competition: Is a sliding scale of 0-1. The closer to "1" the keyword is, the more competitive the keyword phrase is and the more people there are bidding on that keyword phrase. The closer to "0" the keyword is, the less competitive and fewer people there are bidding on that keyword
      iii. Global Monthly Search Volume: Is a bit of a misnomer and slightly misleading. This is actually refers to the number of Adwords impressions shown for a given query, not the number of times the query was typed in. "-1" does not mean that there is no search volume for a given term, it simply means that the term has had negligible traffic and not consistent enough for Google to place a value.
         Tip: Google KWT automatically displays values with "broad" match, meaning that it incorporates **ALL queries** in which the target phrase could be used, providing inflated numbers. To get a more accurate picture, select "Exact" under match-type.

4. **Select keywords that accurately describe your product/content**
   Tip: try to select no more than 2-3 keyword phrases per category and sub-category

The Competitive Marketplace Evaluation

As mentioned, perhaps one of the first challenges to properly defining web content is the inevitable internal struggle between the competing interests within a company. In particular, this is true of mid- to large-sized corporations with clearly defined departments, executive managers, and objectives and roles for each. Hence, everyone is an expert when it comes to their own department, to managing the corporate image, sales messaging, and presentation.

Agree or not, it is a struggle that must be resolved through compromise. Logical arguments confirmed with statistics and proof will go a long way towards co-opting the naysayers and strategy outliers. Although it can be painful at first, this s the perfect opportunity to thoroughly familiarize yourself with not only Internet market data (online research), but more importantly with onsite statistics from the existing analytics on your current website (because you already have it there, of course).

Q: Why is a competitive evaluation the next step?
A: In many cases, it can be an enormous time-saver. Knowing what your competition is doing can often be of great help in defining what you must do and how you want to position yourself; however, this is not always the case.

Keep in mind, that when we say "competition" we mean your direct competitors in the search engines--**those vying for the web marketplace**. These are the ones who really matter as regards your search marketing efforts. All too often when we ask for a competitor list from clients, they provide us with companies that have been traditional adversaries over the years (i.e. John Doe's XYZ company located in a nearby city or town), and often don't have a substantial web presence, or no web presence at all. **We are not concerned with them**. We want to know who is forging ahead in the search marketplace, both from an SEO and a PPC standpoint. In a matter of minutes, you can have enough perspective to know how difficult it is going to be to obtain front-page exposure for the most desirable keywords.

All of the factors we have previously discussed about building an effective website and brand presence online come into play here. Reading through the list below may sound overwhelming and confusing, but have no fear: with some practice, you will be able to evaluate your competitors' websites in a matter of a few minutes apiece.

Defining Your Keywords, Current Rankings, and Backlinks

1. What are your Primary Market Keywords?
   - ❖ Google's Traffic Estimator
        a. Primary KW's - Define the Top 10-20 keywords your site must rank for
        b. Include Google's
             i. CPC estimations
             ii. Percentage of Competition
             iii. Local and/or Global traffic values
2. Does your site currently rank for its primary keywords?
   - ❖ SEM Rush -
        Add any keywords that you are aware of, not in the SEM Rush database

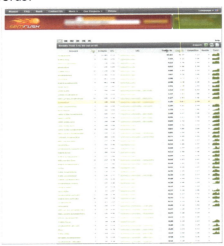

2. What is the state of your Current Backlinks?
   - ❖ Yahoo Site Explorer, SEOMoz's LinkScape, or Link Diagnosis
        c. Run a full linking diagnosis on your site
        d. What websites are linking to yours?
        e. What are the Anchor Texts?

Defining Your Current Website Traffic and Conversions

1. Are these keywords relevant to traffic results?
   - ❖ Google Analytics
        Are you seeing any traffic from the keywords you rank for?
2. Where is your current traffic coming from?
   - ❖ Google Analytics
        a. Traffic Sources Overview
             i. Keyword Traffic Report
             ii. Search Engine Traffic Report
        b. Geo-Mapping report

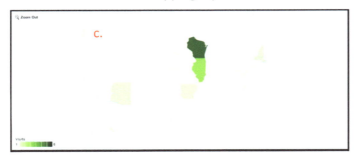

a. Referring Sites report

	Visits 538 % of Site Total 70.14%	Pages/Visit 3.24 Site Avg 3.20 (1.36%)	Avg. Time on Site 00:02:38 Site Avg 00:02:09 (22.09%)	% New Visits 80.30% Site Avg 79.66% (0.80%)	Bounce Rate 0.19% Site Avg 0.52% (-64.36%)
	Source	None	Visits ↓	Pages/Visit	Avg. Time on Site	% New Visits	Bounce Rate

#	Source	Visits	Pages/Visit	Avg. Time on Site	% New Visits	Bounce Rate
1	facebook.com	348	3.36	00:03:17	82.18%	0.00%
2	aweber.com	63	2.92	00:00:52	96.83%	0.00%
3	ettms-journal.blogspot.com	21	4.05	00:02:07	71.43%	4.76%
4	abcnews.go.com	20	2.70	00:01:32	45.00%	0.00%
5	us.mc458.mail.yahoo.com	15	2.07	00:00:01	13.33%	0.00%
6	m.facebook.com	8	2.00	00:00:01	87.50%	0.00%
7	twitter.com	5	4.00	00:12:56	60.00%	0.00%
8	v.mc287.mail.yahoo.com	3	2.00	00:00:01	33.33%	0.00%
9	linkedin.com	3	2.33	00:00:14	66.67%	0.00%
10	spiritbar.wm120.mail.live.com	3	4.00	00:01:22	33.33%	0.00%

3. What are they doing when they come to your site?
   ❖ Google Analytics
      a. Site Usage Statistics:
         i. Pageviews
         ii. Bounce Rate
         iii. Average Time on site
         iv. Downloads (PDF's, etc)

4. Currently, are your conversion opportunities clearly defined?
   ❖ Manual Evaluation of your site
      a. Is a "Contact Us" page your only online conversion opportunity?
      b. Does your "Contact Us" form require too much information?
      c. Do you have a "Quick Contact" form on every page of the site?
      d. Do you offer a newsletter, RSS feed, Twitter account, or some other form of recurring communication?
      e. Do you have concise calls to action on your homepage and internal pages of the site?
      f. Have you created a user path structure on your site, to guide your audience down predetermined paths?
      g. Are there any "dead ends" on your site? Places where it is difficult to navigate out of?

5. What are your current Goal Conversion Numbers and the Conversion Ratio?
   ❖ Google Analytics – Custom Report
      a. Assuming your Goals have been setup correctly, you will be able to determine actual conversion values
      b. Setup a report defining Conversion against:
         i. Source/Medium
         ii. Keyword

6. What is your current Cost Per Conversion?
   ❖ Google Analytics
   ❖ Manual
      a. This will only be obtainable directly through GA if you are engaged in an AdWords PPC campaign

b. What are you currently spending on advertising, email marketing, trade shows, etc?

Defining the Competitiveness of Your Marketplace

Who are your Top Competitors in Search?
- ❖ SEM Rush
  a. The SEM Rush dashboard includes a report on other websites that are competing for the same kw's that you are currently ranked for.
  b. If you have a PPC campaign, they will also provide a report showing your direct competitors
- ❖ SEO Quake
  a. Run your top 5-10 keywords through Google, with SEO Quake turned on
  b. This provides a fantastic set of stats that allows you to compare your website side by side with your direct competitors'
- ❖ Link Diagnosis
  a. Do they have good keywords as Anchor Text Links?
  b. What are the PR values for the pages linking to their site?
  c. Who is linking to them?

2. What Keywords do they Rank for, and how many are there?
- ❖ SEM Rush
- ❖ SEO Quake

3. Do they have an effective conversion strategy on their site?
- ❖ Manual Evaluation

Build a ranking evaluation – to score competitors on a scale of 1-10
- Look at their site for keywords in these locations:
  - Page Titles:
    - Are these competitor sites using keyword phrases within title tags?
    - Do the title tags have consistency (eg., all using pipe delimiters or dashes)
    - Is there over-optimization? (eg., multiple uses--4 times or more--of the targeted keyword?)
    - How is the title tag structured? (Does the title tag follow site hierarchy or is company name first followed by targeted keywords?)
  - Meta Descriptions
    - Is competitor using keyword phrases within the meta-description?
    - Is competitor using keyword phrases within the meta-keywords tag? *(NOTE: the meta-keywords tag is of no value algorithmically to search engines and NOT used as a ranking factor by any of the major engines)*
  - Navigation and Menus
    - Is the competitor using full targeted keyword phrases within their navigation and menus? Or are they using a jargon within the navigation and menu?
    - Is the competitor employing breadcrumb navigation? Is the breadcrumb navigation employing full keyword phrase use?
  - Page Headers

- Is the competitor employing heading tags within the content? (eg., h1 and h2 tags?)
- Is the competitor employing keyword phrases within the content tastefully? That is, does it appear to be forced or is it a natural placement?
  - o Text links in the content
    - Is the competitor using hypertext links within the body content that links to other internal content on the website?
    - Is the hypertext link using targeted keyword and phrase text as the anchor?
- Using SEO Quake:
  - o How many links are listed from Yahoo?
    - Quantity of links is important; general guideline is the more links you have the better
    - Also important is the QUALITY of those links. Are links that are coming back to the website on-topic, relevant to what the site does, and trusted links?
    - Example for Quality Links: a site has 100,000 links coming back to it. Of those links, 50,000 are coming from "bad neighborhoods" (i.e. porn websites, online pharmacy websites, or link farms). In this case half or more of the links this site has are NOT relevant, on-topic, and trustworthy.
  - o How old is their site?
    - Domain age is a key indicator to a site's trust and relevance with the search engines
    - General guideline: The older a website is (in terms of domain age), the more trust and relevance it will have. However, this is not always the case, as new sites with great, very linkable content can and will be considered very trustworthy.
  - o Do they have links from Yahoo, DMOZ, Best of the Web, and Business.com directories?
    - These links come from very powerful domains in their own right, and because three of the four are paid directories, they establish (through link juice and the provider domain's trust and relevance) that the receiving website should be considered relevant and trustworthy.
- Using SEM Rush:
  - o How many keywords do they rank for in the top 20?
    - As we have already stated, SEM Rush is geared toward pulling long-tail keywords as well as broad, general keywords. Therefore, the guideline here is that the more keyword phrases a website ranks for, per SEM Rush, it is a very good indicator that the competitor site is very indexable by search engines and supplies relevant and trustworthy content for the end-user.
  - o Are their rankings for a mixture of brand and product, or just brand?
    - If you see that the majority of the keyword phrases a competitor site ranks for is brand-oriented, then you can reasonably assume that the competitor is doing very little in terms of search engine marketing or optimization.
    - Ideally, with your own site as well, you'll want to see a solid blend of product keyword phrases and brand-oriented keywords

How to Build a Competitive Market Evaluation

The best approach, without getting overwhelmed, is to pick your top 3-5 Keywords. We recommend this approach as C-Level executives have an overwhelming tendency to want to focus on every possible keyword. Additionally, culling a list down to 3-5 keywords, allows you to focus on what really matters to your business and not become hung up on things that are inconsequential in the grand scheme of things.

We suggest looking at keyword phrases that impact the bottom-line of the business, whether this is a particularly profitable service you offer, a product that provides excellent margins, or a product/service line that you want to establish in the future. It is more important as this point to focus on keyword phrases that help to propel the bottom-line forward as opposed to company name or brand-orientated phrases. In a majority of cases, brand keywords and phrases take care of themselves.

The best tools for this are:

- Google's Toolbar, with Page Rank turned "on"
  - Please note: This is updated infrequently by Google. Use this as a gauge to assess a website's trust, authority, and relevancy.
- Google's Keyword Tool
  - Use the "website content" option on the left-hand side
  - This is will generate possible, though on many occasions not very accurate, list keywords and phrases that a competitor could target based on the content of their website
  - Export keywords to .csv file
- SEO Quake, a plug-in tool for your Mozilla/Firefox browser and Google's Chrome browser
  - After you have installed the plug-in, you will need to go to "Preferences" and "Advanced" to adjust how SEO Quake will retrieve this information. As noted in the sections above, SEO Quake uses your IP address to retrieve this information, and if it is not adjusted properly, will cause your IP to be seen as a spam-robot, in turn causing Google to block that IP address.
  - We recommend setting the Parameter Requests to 3000 (or more) ms, this will provide enough of a gap between calls as to seem "normal" to the search engines
  - Use Google and search for your desired keyword
  - Allow for the parameters to fully load into the SERP (search engine result page)
  - Save this SERP to a folder on your laptop's/computer's hard drive
  - Once this has saved, you can search for another keyword phrase

Once you have completed your searches, access these saved files from SEO Quake. The information captured from the SERPs will be displayed for you, and you can begin your comparison of the top ten sites that rank for the particular keyword of interest. Your finished result should look something like this:

Keyword: Printed Circuit Boards										
Url	Google pagerank	Google index	Google cachedate	Yahoo links	Yahoo linkdomain	Yahoo dir	Dmoz	Webarchive age	Robots.txt	Sitemap.xml
http://en.wikipedia.org/wiki/Printed_circuit_board	6	3770000	31-Dec-08	1161	86978080	10253	10000	Nov 27 2002	yes	no
http://www.expresspcb.com/	6	36	2-Jan-09	3416	4357	1	2	Nov 11 1998	no	no
http://www.lvr.com/pcbs.htm	4	153	1-Jan-09	39	6999	3	3	Dec 20 1996	no	no
http://www.youtube.com/watch?v=urv6jArKp6M	4	662000000	6-Jan-09	46	135583731	131	261	Apr 28 2005	yes	no
http://www.robotroom.com/PCB.html	4	260	2-Jan-09	88	8955	No	1	Sep 26 2000	yes	no
http://www.4pcb.com/	5	419	6-Jan-09	1644	2026	1	1	Jan 25 1999	no	yes
http://www.epa.gov/dfe/pubs/projects/pcb/index.htm	5	983000	23-Nov-08	52	1671049	141	516	Apr 18 1997	yes	no
http://www.circuitworld.com/subpage/pcbfab.htm	4	43	23-Dec-08	32	1003	1	1	Oct 31 1996	no	no
http://www.pcbexpress.com/	5	102	2-Jan-09	20294	20532	1	2	Dec 24 1997	no	no
http://www.onboardcircuits.com/	3	8	1-Jan-09	361	444	No	No	Mar 24 2004	no	no

Appendix:

Content Management Systems

Over the past few years, a plethora of fairly user friendly, self-administered website systems have become available. They represent the latest generation of website technology and offer numerous benefits over "static" HTML websites. While this development was initially driven by the blogosphere and was dominated by platforms developed in the PHP programming language, a decent number of ASP.NET (Microsoft) systems have come to fruition, not to mention droves of proprietary ("Hosted") systems offered by private companies.

There are some baseline phrases you should know and understand before diving into the following.

- *Portal* – A portal is a fancy way of saying website. You should be aware that the term "portal" has in recent years taken on additional connotations relating to social networking communities (or websites that are far more "involved" or "complex" than a typical business' website).
- *Front-end* – The "front end" of a website is the publicly viewable portion of a website. The pages that can be seen and interacted with by anyone visiting the site.
- *Back-end* – The "Back-end" of a website refers to the portion of a website that is password protected and accessed by website administrators to add/edit/delete content visible on the publicly-facing front end.
- *Content Management System (or CMS)* – CMS indicates that website administrators have flexibility to add/edit/delete content found on a website on-the-fly or "in real time." That is, changes made in the administrative Back-end of a website are reflected instantaneously on the publicly visible front-end of the site. It is important to note that this does not mean that a typical administrative user can change all aspects of a given site. Rather, CMS platforms are primarily concerned with granting flexibility to content that is given to change frequently. Examples would be News Stories, Press Releases, Sales Rep Directories, Corporate Events, Blog posts, etc.
- *Open Source* – "Open Source" in the most widely accepted use of the term refers to foundational code that can be modified to a significant extent. In some respects it is easier to speak of what Open Source isn't rather than is. For example, if you purchase a license for Microsoft Word and load it onto your laptop, you may use the product, but you cannot access or change the code upon which the word processor software runs. Likewise, if you use Adobe Photoshop, you do not have access to the code behind the application. You cannot modify the code to your liking in order to add or suppress additional functionality as you see fit. Likewise, you cannot change functionality to work this way when it was programmed to work in a different way. Preferences can be changed, but only those preferences offered out-of-the-box by the authoring company. Open Source solutions enable programmers to "open" and amend code as needed and at will. There are, of course, limits to the degree and depth of access in most cases, but there are very few restrictions. So, it is entirely possible for an adept programmer to modify the out-of-the-box code provided on install to the degree that it is, for all intents and purposes, barely recognizable as having started out as a normative installation.

"Open Source" also refers to the predominance of "open user licenses" for the more well-known Open Source solutions. Open Source source code is free for the taking, meaning that a developer can download an "instance" of a given open source solution without having to pay a licensing fee to do so.

And then, the developer can slice and dice the code as he/she sees fit. It should be noted here that it common for Open Source solutions providers to offer a "community" edition (free of licensing concerns) and a more robust "commercial" version (usually involving licensing costs). Commercial editions are typically more flexible, entail a degree of professional support, and/or offer additional functionality not found and/or supported in the commensurate Community Edition.

"Open Source" also entails the concept of "community development"; that is, while core functionality of a given Open Source solution might be officially managed by a small group of developers, an active community of "devotee" programmers is involved in developing additional plug-ins, variations to functionality, extensions to existing functionality, new interesting solutions that retrofit or integrate into a given Open Source platform, fixes, work-arounds, and all manner of "tweaks" one might think of to the "sanctioned" out-of-the-box version.

Each of the Open Source solutions below has extremely active communities of developers, located throughout the entire world, who are constantly engaged in altering, modifying, and authoring code relating to the solution(s) they are fluent in.

One word of caution: It is important to note that an Open Source solution (or platform) may be written in the same primary coding language (programming language) as another. But, even so, each platform has its own peculiarities. So, simply because you have a PHP coder, for instance, who is fluent in Drupal, one should not assume he/she is fluent in Joomla! (although both are PHP-based solutions). It is safer to say that a PHP coder who is fluent in Drupal speaks Portuguese, while a PHP coder who is fluent in Joomla! speaks Spanish. A native speaker of one will have a much easier time learning the other than a speaker of German may, but even so it could take some time to do so.

Platform vs Solution – sometimes the term "platform" means different things to different people. It is safe to refer to a given Open Source CMS "brand" as a "platform." But it is safer still to refer to it as a "solution." The reason for this is that IT people in particular use "platform" to mean an entirely different thing than a typical programmer might.

Another cautionary note to the reader: the analysis below is our attempt to capture a snapshot of the competitive strengths and weaknesses of the major Open Source CMS solutions in the marketplace as of this writing. But, as with all things web, the material may now be dated. The marketplace moves at an incredibly rapid pace. So, it is crucial to make sure that you have up-to-the present day information, as the generalizations below may or may not be current at the time you read this.

The following list is meant to provide you with some options, and discuss the strengths and weaknesses of each system. We have included our personal recommendations based on direct experience.

Notes: the scoring that follows is subjective, but based on the best widely available information and our own professional experiences with each of the platforms represented. In the end analysis, the best advice we can give you is to find a competent, trusted Interactive Project Manager/Information Architect and ask him/her to analyze which platform makes the best sense for the project at hand. Keep in mind each project is different. Each set of requirements and business objectives is distinct. So proceed with due diligence and an open mind. Averages are *not* weighted.

Content Management System (Platform) Matrix

NOTE = As of Summer, 2009 – These things can change very RAPIDLY.

Scale: 1-5 (5 = best)	Drupal	DotNetNuke	Joomla!	WordPress	MODx
Official Website	Drupal.org	DotNetNuke.com	Joomla.org	WordPress.org	MODx.com
Commercial-Grade eCommerce	★★★★★	★★★★★	★★★☆☆	★★☆☆☆	★☆☆☆☆
Commercial Grade Non-eComm Product Catalog/RFQ	★★★☆☆	★★★☆☆	★★☆☆☆	★☆☆☆☆	★☆☆☆☆
Informational Only	★★★☆☆	★★★★☆	★★☆☆☆	★★★★★	★★★★☆
Blog Only	★★☆☆☆	★★★☆☆	★★☆☆☆	★★★★★	★☆☆☆☆
	Drupal is a free software package that allows an individual or a community of users to easily publish, manage and organize a wide variety of content on a website. Tens of thousands of people and organizations are using Drupal to power scores of different web sites, including Community web portals, Discussion sites, Corporate web sites, Intranet applications, Personal web sites or blogs, Aficionado sites, E-commerce applications, Resource directories, Social Networking sites.

Drupal is ready to go from the moment you | The DotNetNuke Community Edition is the most widely used web content management system and application development framework for Microsoft .NET. More than 400,000 highly interactive, dynamic web sites worldwide are built on the DotNetNuke Community Edition. The DotNetNuke Community Edition allows users to easily create and manage their web site or web application through any common web browser. Very easy to use, new content contributors can learn to add or modify content in minutes. Administrators will find the application very easy to manage on a standard Microsoft stack running Windows Server, IIS, and Microsoft SQL. The | Joomla! is a powerful Open Source Content Management System for building professional web sites easily. It is often the system of choice for small business or home users who want a professional looking site that's simple to deploy and use. It can deliver a robust enterprise-level Web site as well, empowered by endless extensibility for your bespoke publishing needs. Joomla! is different from the normal models for content management software. For starters, it's not complicated. Joomla! has been developed for everybody, and anybody can develop it further. Similarly to the Firefox browser, | WordPress is a state-of-the-art semantic personal publishing platform with a focus on aesthetics, web standards, and usability. What a mouthful. WordPress is both free and priceless at the same time. More simply, Wordpress is what you use when you want to work with your blogging software, not fight it. N.B.: WordPress' default capabilities can be increased many fold (and new functions can be easily added) through its easy-to-use plugin architecture. [cmsmatrix.com] | MODx is an open source PHP Application Framework that helps you take control of your online content. It empowers developers and advanced users to give as much control as desired to whomever they desire for day-to-day website content maintenance chores. [cmsmatrix.com] |

	download it. It even has an easy-to-use web installer! The built-in functionality, combined with dozens of freely available add-on modules, will enable features such as Content Management Systems, Blogs, Collaborative authoring environments, Forums, Peer-to-peer networking, Newsletters, Podcasting, Picture galleries, File uploads and downloads, and much more. Drupal is open-source software distributed under the GPL ("GNU General Public License") and is maintained and developed by a community of thousands of users and developers. If you like what Drupal promises for you, please work with us to expand and refine Drupal to suit your specific needs. [cmsmatrix.com]	Community Edition is a highly extensible, scalable framework. It enables organizations to easily add to their web site by building or purchasing "modules" for additional functionality or "skins" to control its look and feel. The DotNetNuke Community Edition is supported by hundreds of module vendors worldwide that have created thousands of affordable extensions for the framework. The DotNetNuke Community Edition is supported by a worldwide ecosystem with over 700,000 registered members and thousands of system integrators, design firms, and hosting companies. [cmsmatrix.com]	the core system can be extended via easily installable add-ons authored by the developer community. The comprehensive internationalization of Joomla! 1.5.x supports right to left languages (eg. Hebrew or Arabic) and extended character sets. Dozens of language packs can be separately downloaded. [cmsmatrix.com]		
Maturity	2000	2002	2001	2003	2004
License Type	GNU (General Public License - free) The Drupal system is free and requires no licensing fees, no per-user fees and no yearly maintenance fees.	BSD-style (free). The DotNetNuke system is free and requires no licensing fees, no per-user fees and no yearly maintenance fees.	GNU (General Public License - free) The Joomla! system is free and requires no licensing fees, no per-user fees and no yearly maintenance fees.	GNU (General Public License - free) The WordPress system is free and requires no licensing fees, no per-user fees and no yearly maintenance fees.	GNU (General Public License - free) The MODx system is free and requires no licensing fees, no per-user fees and no yearly maintenance fees.
Language	PHP	ASP.NET	PHP	PHP	PHP

Hosting Requirements	Drupal	DotNetNuke	Joomla!	WordPress	MODx
Operating System	Platform Independent	MS Windows	Platform Independent	Platform Independent	Platform Independent
Server	Apache / IIS	IIS	Apache / IIS	Apache / IIS	Apache / IIS
Database	MySQL	MSSQL	MySQL	MySQL	MySQL
Editions	Community	Community and Professional	Community	Community	Community

Platform Marketplace Strength	Drupal	DotNetNuke	Joomla!	WordPress	MODx
Volume of Site Deployments	★★★☆☆	★★☆☆☆	★★★★☆	★★★★★	★☆☆☆☆
Volume of Downloads	★★★★☆	★★★☆☆	★★★★★	★★★★★	★☆☆☆☆
Size of Developer Community	★★★★☆	★★★☆☆	★★★★★	★★★★★	★☆☆☆☆
Prevalence of Add-On Modules	★★★★☆	★★★☆☆	★★★★★	★★★★★	★☆☆☆☆
Commercial Training	★★★★☆	★★★★★	★★★☆☆	★☆☆☆☆	★☆☆☆☆
Commercial Support	★★★★☆	★★★★★	★★★☆☆	★☆☆☆☆	★☆☆☆☆
Commercial Manuals	★★★★★	★★★★☆	★★★★☆	★☆☆☆☆	★☆☆☆☆
User Conferences	★★★★★	★★★★★	★★★★★	★★★★★	★☆☆☆☆
Administrative Usability	★★★☆☆	★★★★☆	★☆☆☆☆	★★★★★	★★★☆☆
Commercial-grade eComm	★★★★★	★★★★★	★★★☆☆	★☆☆☆☆	★☆☆☆☆

Affordability	Drupal	DotNetNuke	Joomla!	WordPress	MODx
Entry	★★★★☆	★★★☆☆	★★★★★	★★★★★	★★★★☆
Programming & Development	★★★★☆	★★★☆☆	★★★★★	★★★★★	★★★★☆
Hosting	★★★★☆	★★★☆☆	★★★★★	★★★★★	★★★★★
Maintenance & Updates	★★★★☆	★★★☆☆	★★★☆☆	★★★★★	★★★★☆

SEM - Strategic Comparison Matrix

Strategy	Rationale	Expense Frequency	Relative Cost in Dollars	Relative Cost in Effort	Cost of Inaction (opportunity cost of doing nothing)	Impact Horizon	
PPC Advertising	Increases Quantity of Leads via Increasing Site Traffic via Paid Inclusion in Search Engine "Results"	Ongoing Expense	High	High	Variable	Immediate	Though relatively costly, can garner immediate results in terms of traffic. However, the moment you stop advertising is the moment you stop benefitting from PPC.
Link-Building	Increases Quantity of Leads via Increasing Traffic via Increasing Site's rank in the Search Engines	Periodic Expense	Low	High	Variable	Long-Term	Can be regarded as an advertising cost, especially for directory listings that need to be renewed. On the other hand, many links are a one-time investment, requiring no annual subscription fee.
Onsite SEO	Increases Quantity of Leads via Increasing Traffic via Increasing Site's rank in the Search Engines	Periodic Expense	Moderate	High	High	Long-Term	Requiring time and patience, but delivering long-term benefits in the form of increased traffic and liberating you to some extent from the expense of ongoing PPC advertising.
Lead Capture Optimization	Increases Quantity of Leads via Improving/Including On-site Lead Capture Mechanisms	One-Time Expense	Low	Low	High	Immediate	When compared to PPC and SEO, LCO is an extremely low-cost endeavor which can increase the amount of leads harvested from a website exponentially. In addition, LCO is similar to PPC in the sense that results are instantaneous. It is dissimilar in that it is *not* an advertising expense, and does *not* include ongoing recurring costs.
User Path Optimization	Increases Quantity of Leads via Improving the usability of a site, guiding specific types of users to specific calls-to-action	One-Time Expense	Moderate	Moderate	High	Immediate	In some cases only nominal changes are required. In other cases, the necessary remedy may be revamping the entirety of the site (a new site altogether). Nevertheless, a site which is nonsensical to visitors or even marginally difficult to navigate or make sense of from the visitor's standpoint can impede profits in untold ways.
Cross Promotion	Increases Quantity of Leads via Increasing Site Traffic via Inclusion in ongoing advertising outlays	One-Time Expense	Low	Low	Variable	Immediate	Simply the "art" of maximizing your site's exposure via already paid-for channels, such as newsletters, business cards, on-hold messages,

							voicemail greetings, email signatures, invoices, and the like.
Increasing Sales Conversion %	Increases Closing percentage of Leads	NA	Moderate	High	High	Mid-Term	The analysis relating to diagnosing where problems exist and the effort it takes to remedy them can require a good deal of time, effort, training, and discipline. However, the costs associated with doing nothing in this regard are often significantly higher than taking action to correct a less-than-optimal situation. In this sense, one should consider this an ongoing internal project.
Increase Net Profit per Transaction	Increases profit	NA	Low	High	Variable	Mid-Term	Also requires a good deal of analysis, from personnel to sales methodology. In some cases, the time investment is minimal. In other cases, the exercise can reveal massive inefficiencies.
Decrease Expense per Transaction	Increases profit	NA	Low	High	Variable	Mid-Term	Increasing Net Profit by another name

Content and Keyword Layering Pyramid

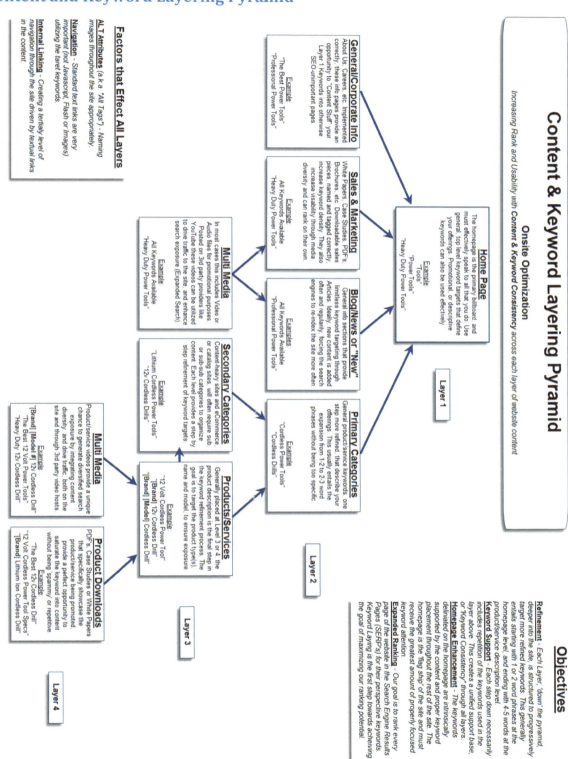

Content & Keyword Layering Pyramid

Onsite Optimization

Increasing Rank and Usability with Content & Keyword Consistency across each layer of website content

Layer 1

Home Page
The homepage is the primary billboard and must effectively speak to all that you do. Use general, top level keyword targets that define your offerings. Promotional or descriptive keywords can also be used effectively
Example
"Tools"
"Power Tools"
"Heavy Duty Power Tools"

General/Corporate Info
About Us, Careers, etc. Implemented correctly, these info pages provide an opportunity to "Content Stuff" your Layer 1 Keywords into otherwise SEO-unimportant pages
Example
"The Best Power Tools"
"Professional Power Tools"

Sales & Marketing
White Papers, Case Studies, PDF's, Brochures, etc. Downloadable sales pieces, named and tagged correctly, increase keyword density. They also increase visability through media diversity and can rank on their own
Example
All Keywords Available
"Heavy Duty Power Tools"

Blog/News or "New"
General info sections that provide limitless keyword targeting through Articles. Ideally, new content is added often and regularly, forcing the search engines to re-index the site more often
Examples
All Keywords Available
"Professional Power Tools"

Multi Media
In most cases this includes Video or Audio files for promotional purposes. Posted on 3rd party providers like YouTube these videos can be utilized to drive traffic to the site and enhance search exposure (Expanded Search)
Example
All Keywords Available
"Heavy Duty Power Tools"

Layer 2

Primary Categories
General product/service keywords, one step more refined, that describe your offerings. This usually entails the expansion from 1-2 to 2-3 word phrases without being too specific.
Example
"Cordless Power Tools"
"Cordless Drills"

Secondary Categories
Content-heavy sites and eCommerce or catalog sites will often require sub or sub-sub categories to organize content. Each level provides a step by step refinement of keyword targets
Example
"Lithium Cordless Power Tools"
"12v Cordless Drills"

Layer 3

Products/Services
Generally placed at Level 3 or 4, the product description is the final step in the keyword refinement process. The goal is to target the product type(s), name and model, to ensure exposure
Example
"12 Volt Cordless Power Tool"
"[Brand] 12v Cordless Drill"
"[Brand] [Model] Cordless Drill"

Multi Media
Product/service videos provide a unique chance to generate diversified search exposure by integrating content diversity, and drive traffic, both on site and through 3rd party video hosts
Example
"[Brand] [Model #] 12v Cordless Drill"
"The Best 12 Volt Power Tools"
"Heavy Duty 12v Cordless Drill"

Layer 4

Product Downloads
PDF's, Case Studies or White Papers that specifically showcase the product/service being promoted, provide a perfect opportunity to saturate the keyword into content without being "spammy" or repetitive
Example
"The Best 12v Cordless Drill"
"12 Volt Cordless Power Tool Specs"
"[Brand] Lithium Ion Cordless Drill"

Objectives

Refinement - Each Layer, 'down' the pyramid, deeper into the site, is structured to progressively target more refined keywords. This generally entails starting with 1 or 2 word phrases at the homepage level, and ending with 4-5 words at the product/service description level.

Keyword Support - Each step down necessarily includes repetition of the keywords used in the layer above. This creates a unified support base, or "Keyword Consistency" through all layers.

Homepage Enhancement - The keywords delineated on the homepage are intrinsically supported throughout the content and proper keyword placement throughout the rest of the site. The homepage is the "flag ship" of the site and must receive the greatest amount of properly focused keyword attention.

Expanded Ranking - Our goal is to rank every page of the website in the Search Engine Results Pages (SERP's) for their perspective keywords. Keyword Layering is the first step towards achieving the goal of maximizing our ranking potential.

Factors that Effect All Layers

ALT Attributes (a.k.a. "Alt Tags") - Naming images throughout the site appropriately.

Navigation - Standard text links are very important (not Javascript, Flash or Images) utilizing the taret keywords.

Internal Linking - Creating a tertialy level of navigation through the site driven by textual links in the content.

The Benefits of Web Analytics

Links – Inbound & Outbound

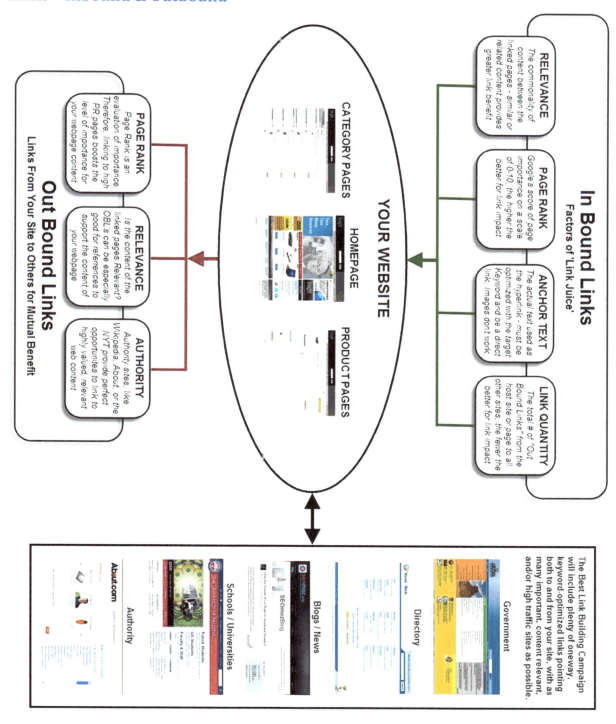

Optimized Backlink Pyramid

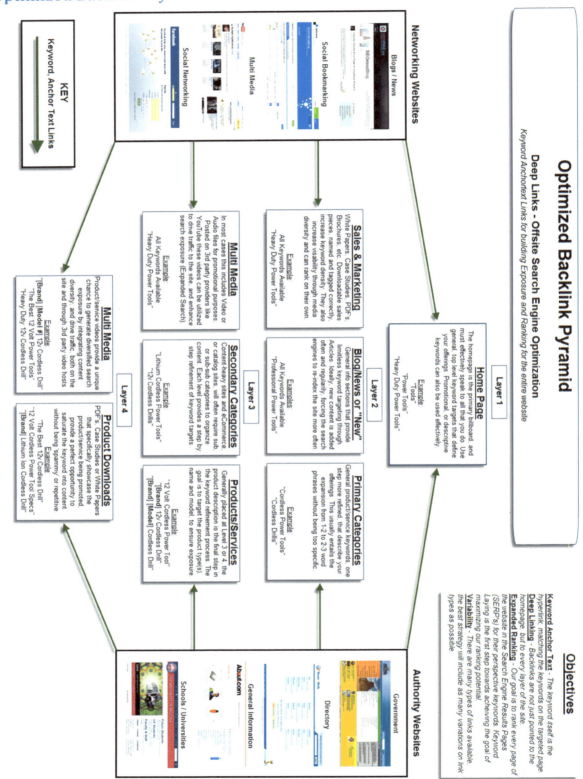

Optimized Backlink Pyramid

Deep Links - Offsite Search Engine Optimization

Keyword Anchortext Links for building Exposure and Ranking for the entire website

KEY
Keyword, Anchor Text Links

Networking Websites

Blogs / News

Social Networking

Multi Media

Social Bookmarking

Layer 1

Home Page
The homepage is the primary billboard, and must effectively speak to all that you do. Use general, top level keyword targets that define your offerings. Promotional or descriptive keywords can also be used effectively.

Example:
"Tools"
"Power Tools"
"Heavy Duty Power Tools"

Sales & Marketing
White Papers, Case Studies, PDF's, Brochures, etc. Downloadable sales pieces, named and tagged correctly, increase keyword density. They also increase visability through media diversity and can rank on their own.

Example:
All Keywords Available
"Heavy Duty Power Tools"

Multi Media
In most cases this includes Video or Audio files for promotional purposes. Posted on 3rd party providers like YouTube these videos can be utilized to drive traffic to the site, and enhance search exposure (Expanded Search).

Example:
All Keywords Available
"Heavy Duty Power Tools"

Layer 2

Blog/News or "New"
General info sections that provide limitless keyword targeting through Articles. Ideally, new content is added often and regularly, forcing the search engines to re-index the site more often.

Examples:
All Keywords Available
"Professional Power Tools"

Secondary Categories
Content-heavy sites and eCommerce or catalog sites will often require sub or sub-sub categories to organize content. Each level provides a step by step refinement of keyword targets.

Example:
"Lithium Cordless Power Tools"
"12v Cordless Drills"

Primary Categories
General product/service keywords, one step more refined, that describe your offerings. This usually entails the expansion from 1-2 to 2-3 word phrases without being too specific.

Example:
"Cordless Power Tools"
"Cordless Drills"

Layer 3

Multi Media
Product/service videos provide a unique chance to generate diversified search exposure, and drive traffic, both on the site and through 3rd party video hosts

Example:
"[Brand] [Model #] 12v Cordless Drill"
"The Best 12 Volt Power Tools"
"Heavy Duty 12v Cordless Drill"

Product Downloads
PDF's, Case Studies or White Papers that specifically showcase the product/service being promoted, provide a perfect opportunity to saturate the keyword into content without being 'spammy' or repetitive

Example:
"The Best 12v Cordless Drill"
"12 Volt Cordless Power Tool Specs"
"[Brand] Lithium Ion Cordless Drill"

Products/Services
Generally placed at Level 3 or 4, the product description is the final step in the keyword refinement process. The goal is to target the product type(s), name and model, to ensure exposure

Example:
"12 Volt Cordless Power Tool"
"[Brand] 12v Cordless Drill"
"[Brand] [Model] Cordless Drill"

Layer 4

Authority Websites

Government

Directory

General Information

Schools / Universities

About.com

Objectives

Keyword Anchor Text - The keyword itself is the hyperlink, matching the keywords on the targeted page.

Deep Linking - Backlinks are not just pointed to the homepage, but to every layer of the site.

Expanded Ranking - Our goal is to rank every page of the website in the Search Engine Results Pages (SERP's), for their perspective keywords. Keyword Laying is the first step towards achieving the goal of maximizing our ranking potential.

Variability - There are many types of links available, the best strategy will include as many variations on link types as possible

Pay-Per-Click Methodology

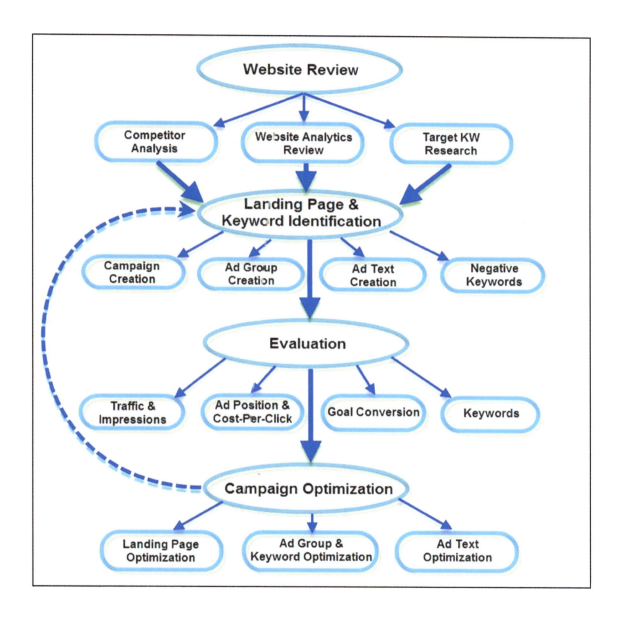

Maximizing ROI and Conversion Rates from PPC

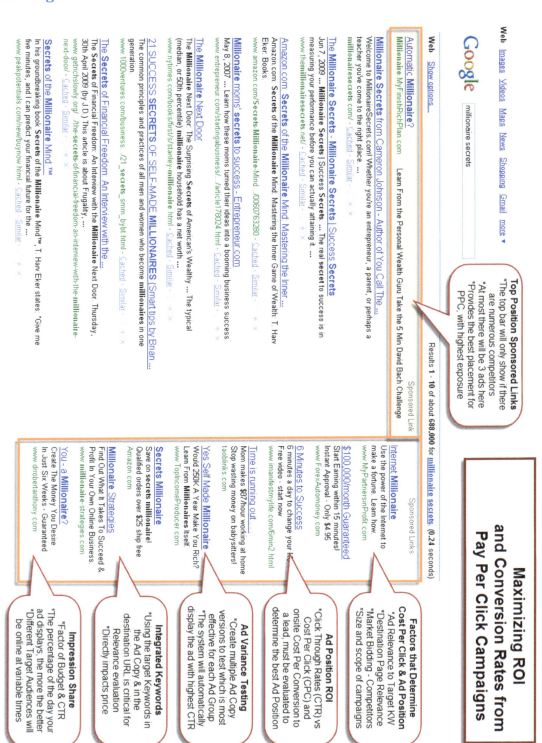

High-Quality Traffic and Exposure Through SEM

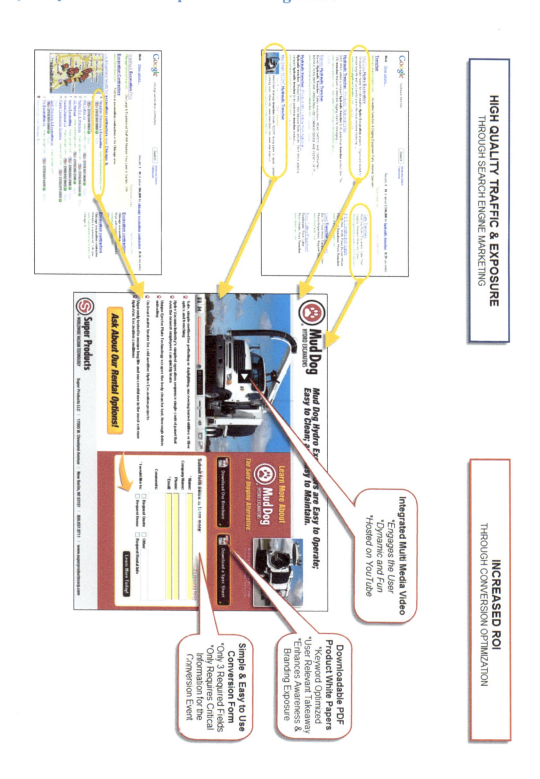

HIGH QUALITY TRAFFIC & EXPOSURE
THROUGH SEARCH ENGINE MARKETING

INCREASED ROI
THROUGH CONVERSION OPTIMIZATION

Integrated Multi Media Video
*Engages the User
*Dynamic and Fun
*Hosted on YouTube

Downloadable PDF
Product White Papers
*Keyword Optimized
*User Relevant Takeaway
*Enhances Awareness &
Branding Exposure

Simple & Easy to Use
Conversion Form
*Only 3 Required Fields
*Only Requires Critical
Information for the
Conversion Event

HIGH QUALITY TRAFFIC & EXPOSURE
THROUGH SEARCH ENGINE MARKETING

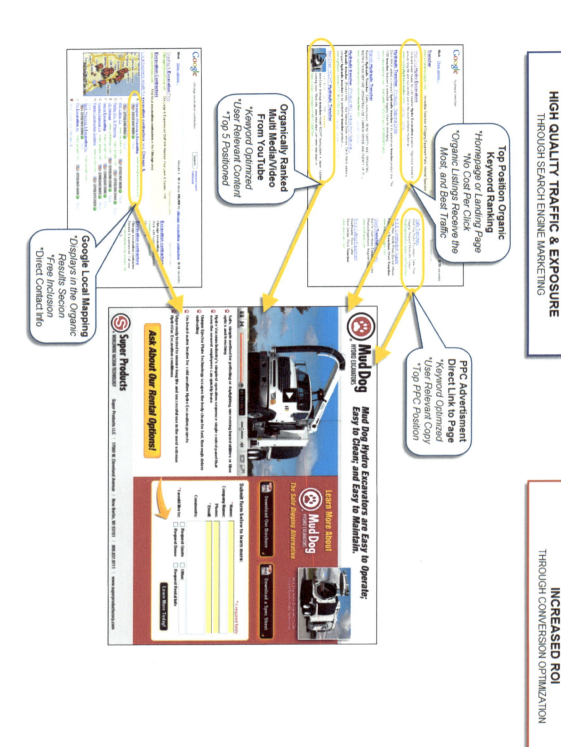

Top Position Organic Keyword Ranking
*Homepage or Landing Page
*No Cost Per Click
*Organic Listings Receive the Most, and Best Traffic

Organically Ranked Multi Media/Video From YouTube
*Keyword Optimized
*User Relevant Content
*Top 5 Positioned

Google Local Mapping
*Displays in the Organic Results Section
*Free Inclusion
*Direct Contact Info

PPC Advertisment Direct Link to Page
*Keyword Optimized
*User Relevant Copy
*Top PPC Position

INCREASED ROI
THROUGH CONVERSION OPTIMIZATION

Easy to Read Text
*Bullet Points
*Bold Type Font
*Keywords Integrated

Clear Calls to Action
*Emboldened
*Highly Visible
*Easy to Understand

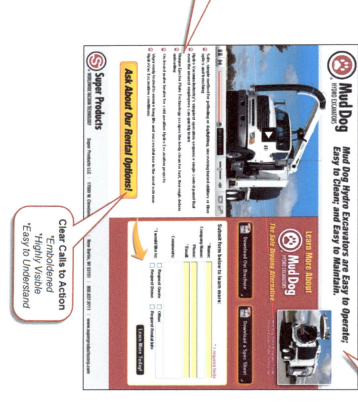

Concise Title
*Clear Statement of Purpose
*Keywords Integrated

INCREASED ROI
THROUGH CONVERSION OPTIMIZATION

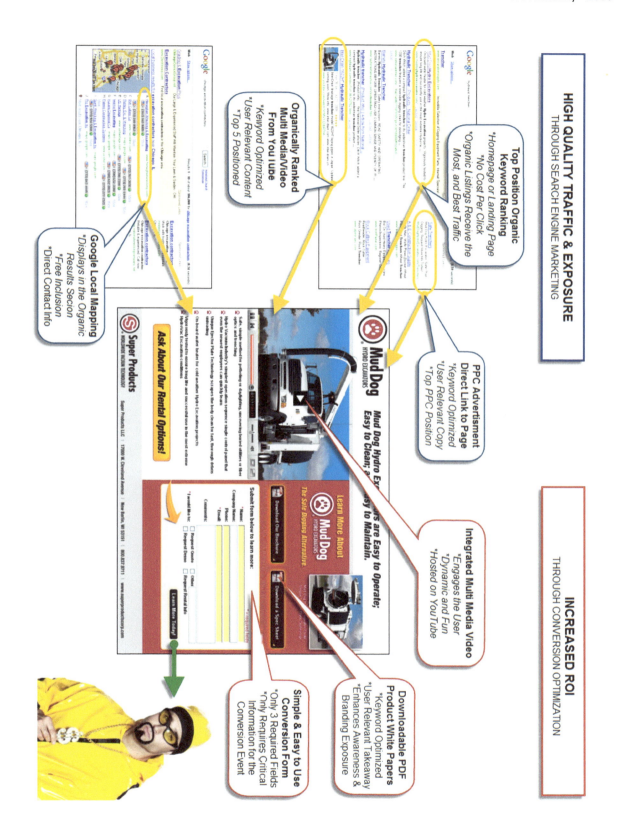

HIGH QUALITY TRAFFIC & EXPOSURE
THROUGH SEARCH ENGINE MARKETING

Top Position Organic Keyword Ranking
*Homepage or Landing Page
*No Cost Per Click
*Organic Listings Receive the Most, and Best Traffic

Organically Ranked Multi Media/Video From YouTube
*User Relevant Content
*Keyword Optimized
*Top 5 Positioned

Google Local Mapping
*Displays in the Organic Results Secion
*Free Inclusion
*Direct Contact Info

PPC Advertisment
Direct Link to Page
*Keyword Optimized
*User Relevant Copy
*Top PPC Position

Integrated Multi Media Video
*Engages the User
*Dynamic and Fun
*Hosted on YouTube

INCREASED ROI
THROUGH CONVERSION OPTIMIZATION

Downloadable PDF Product White Papers
*Keyword Optimized
*User Relevant Takeaway
*Enhances Awareness & Branding Exposure

Simple & Easy to Use Conversion Form
*Only 3 Required Fields
*Only Requires Critical Information for the Conversion Event

www.ingramcontent.com/pod-product-compliance
Lightning Source LLC
Chambersburg PA
CBHW041419050326
40689CB00002B/575